D0899770

Cicero:
Ancient Classics for
English Readers

Rev. W. Lucas Collins

Ancient Classics for English Readers

edited by

REV. W. LUCAS COLLINS, M.A.

CICERO

by

REV. W. LUCAS COLLINS, M.A.

AUTHOR OF 'ETONIANA', 'THE PUBLIC SCHOOLS', ETC.

I have to acknowledge my obligations to Mr. Forsyth's well-known 'Life of Cicero', especially as a guide to the biographical materials which abound in his Orations and Letters. Mr. Long's scholarly volumes have also been found useful. For the translations, such as they are, I am responsible. If I could have met with any which seemed to me more satisfactory, I would gladly have adopted them.

W. L.C.

CONTENTS.

CHAPTER I.

EARLY LIFE AND EDUCATION.

When we speak, in the language of our title-page, of the 'Ancient Classics', we must remember that the word 'ancient' is to be taken with a considerable difference, in one sense. Ancient all the Greek and Roman authors are, as dated comparatively with our modern era. But as to the antique character of their writings, there is often a difference which is not merely one of date. The poetry of Homer and Hesiod is ancient, as having been sung and written when the society in which the authors lived, and to which they addressed themselves, was in its comparative infancy. The chronicles of Herodotus are ancient, partly from their subject-matter and partly from their primitive style. But in this sense there are ancient authors belonging to every nation which has a literature of its own. Viewed in this light, the history of Thucydides, the letters and orations of Cicero, are not ancient at all. Bede, and Chaucer, and Matthew of Paris, and Froissart, are far more redolent of antiquity. The several books which make up what we call the Bible are all ancient, no doubt; but even between the Chronicles of the Kings of Israel and the Epistles of St. Paul there is a far wider real interval than the mere lapse of centuries.

In one respect, the times of Cicero, in spite of their complicated politics, should have more interest for a modern reader than most of what is called Ancient History. Forget the date but for a moment, and there is scarcely anything ancient about them. The scenes and actors are modern—terribly modern; far more so than the middle ages of Christendom. Between the times of our own Plantagenets and Georges, for instance, there is a far wider gap, in all but years, than between the consulships of Caesar and Napoleon. The habits of life, the ways of thinking, the family affections, the tastes of the Romans of Cicero's day, were in many respects wonderfully like our own; the political jealousies and rivalries have repeated themselves again and again in the last two or three centuries of Europe: their code of political honour and morality, debased as it was, was not much lower than that which was held by some great statesmen a generation or two before us. Let us be thankful if the most frightful of their vices were the exclusive shame of paganism.

It was in an old but humble country-house, neat the town of Arpinum, under the Volscian hills, that Marcus Tullius Cicero was born, one hundred and six years before the Christian era. The family was of ancient 'equestrian'[1] dignity, but as none of its members had hitherto borne any office of state, it did not rank as 'noble'. His grandfather and his father had borne the same three names—the last an inheritance from some forgotten ancestor, who had either been successful in the cultivation of vetches (*cicer*), or, as less complimentary traditions said, had a wart of that shape upon his nose. The grandfather was still living when the little Cicero was born; a stout old conservative, who had successfully resisted the attempt to introduce vote by ballot into his native town, and hated the Greeks (who were just then coming into fashion) as heartily as his English representative, fifty years ago, might have hated a Frenchman. "The more Greek a man knew", he protested, "the greater rascal he turned out". The father was a man of quiet habits, taking no part even in local politics, given to books, and to the enlargement and improvement of the old family house, which, up to his time, seems not to have been more than a modest grange. The situation (on a small island formed by the little river Fibrenus[2]) was beautiful and romantic; and the love for it, which grew up with the young Cicero as a child, he never lost in the busy days of his manhood. It was in his eyes, he said, what Ithaca was to Ulysses,

"A rough, wild nurse-land, but whose crops are men".

[Footnote 1: The *Equites* were originally those who served in the Roman cavalry; but latterly all citizens came to be reckoned in the class who had a certain property qualification, and who could prove free descent up to their grandfather.]

[Footnote 2: Now known as Il Fiume della Posta. Fragments of Cicero's villa are thought to have been discovered built into the walls of the deserted convent of San Dominico. The ruin known as 'Cicero's Tower' has probably no connection with him.]

There was an aptness in the quotation; for at Arpinum, a few years before, was born that Caius Marius, seven times consul of Rome, who had at least the virtue of manhood in him, if he had few besides.

But the quiet country gentleman was ambitious for his son. Cicero's father, like Horace's, determined to give him the best education in his power; and of course the best education was to be found in

Rome, and the best teachers there were Greeks. So to Rome young Marcus was taken in due time, with his younger brother Quintus. They lodged with their uncle-in-law, Aculeo, a lawyer of some distinction, who had a house in rather a fashionable quarter of the city, and moved in good society; and the two boys attended the Greek lectures with their town cousins. Greek was as necessary a part of a Roman gentleman's education in those days as Latin and French are with us now; like Latin, it was the key to literature (for the Romans had as yet, it must be remembered, nothing worth calling literature of their own); and, like French, it was the language of refinement and the play of polished society. Let us hope that by this time the good old grandfather was gathered peacefully into his urn; it might have broken his heart to have seen how enthusiastically his grandson Marcus threw himself into this newfangled study; and one of those letters of his riper years, stuffed full of Greek terms and phrases even to affectation, would have drawn anything but blessings from the old gentleman if he had lived to hear them read.

Young Cicero went through the regular curriculum—grammar, rhetoric, and the Greek poets and historians. Like many other youthful geniuses, he wrote a good deal of poetry of his own, which his friends, as was natural, thought very highly of at the time, and of which he himself retained the same good opinion to the end of his life, as would have been natural to few men except Cicero. But his more important studies began after he had assumed the 'white gown' which marked the emergence of the young Roman from boyhood into more responsible life—at sixteen years of age. He then entered on a special education for the bar. It could scarcely be called a profession, for an advocate's practice at Rome was gratuitous; but it was the best training for public life; —it was the ready means, to an able and eloquent man, of gaining that popular influence which would secure his election in due course to the great magistracies which formed the successive steps to political power. The mode of studying law at Rome bore a very considerable resemblance to the preparation for the English bar. Our modern law-student purchases his admission to the chambers of some special pleader or conveyancer, where he is supposed to learn his future business by copying precedents and answering cases, and he also attends the public lectures at the Inns of Court. So at Rome the young aspirant was to be found (but at a much earlier hour than would suit the Temple or Lincoln's Inn) in the open hall of some great jurist's House, listening to his opinions given to the throng of clients who crowded there every morning; while his more zealous pupils would accompany him in his stroll in the Forum, and attend his pleadings in the courts or his speeches on the Rostra, either taking down upon their tablets, or storing in their memories, his *dicta* upon legal questions. [1] In such wise Cicero became the pupil of Mucius Scaevola, whose house was called "the oracle of Rome"—scarcely ever leaving his side, as he himself expresses it; and after that great lawyer's death, attaching himself in much the same way to a younger cousin of the same name and scarcely less reputation. Besides this, to arm himself at all points for his proposed career, he read logic with Diodotus the Stoic, studied the action of Esop and Roscius—then the stars of the Roman stage—declaimed aloud like Demosthenes in private, made copious notes, practised translation in order to form a written style, and read hard day and night. He trained severely as an intellectual athlete; and if none of his contemporaries attained such splendid success, perhaps none worked so hard for it. He made use, too, of certain special advantages which were open to him—little appreciated, or at least seldom acknowledged, by the men of his day—the society and conversation of elegant and accomplished women. In Scaevola's domestic circle, where the mother, the daughters, and the grand-daughters successively seem to have been such charming talkers that language found new graces from their lips, the young advocate learnt some of his not least valuable lessons. "It makes no little difference", said he in his riper years, "what style of expression one becomes familiar with in the associations of daily life". It was another point of resemblance between the age of Cicero and the times in which we live—the influence of the "queens of society", whether for good or evil.

[Footnote 1: These *dicta*, or 'opinions', of the great jurists, acquired a sort of legal validity in the Roman law-courts, like 'cases' with us.]

But no man could be completely educated for a public career at Rome until he had been a soldier. By what must seem to us a mistake in the Republican system—a mistake which we have seen made more than once in the late American war—high political offices were necessarily combined with military command. The highest minister of state, consul or praetor, however hopelessly civilian in tastes and antecedents, might be sent to conduct a campaign in Italy or abroad at a few hours' notice. If a man was a heaven-born general, all went well; if not, he had usually a chance of learning in the school of defeat. It was desirable, at all events, that he should have seen what war was in his youth. Young Cicero served his first campaign, at the age of eighteen, under the father of a man whom he was to know only too well in after life—Pompey the Great—and in the division of the army which was commanded by Sylla as lieutenant-general. He bore arms only for a year or two, and probably saw no very arduous service, or we should certainly have beard of it from himself; and he never was in camp again until he took the chief command, thirty-seven years afterwards, as pro-consul in Cilicia. He was at Rome, leading a quiet student-life—happily for himself, too young to be forced or tempted into an active part—during the bloody feuds between Sylla and the younger Marius.

He seems to have made his first appearance as an advocate when he was about twenty-five, in some suit of which we know nothing. Two years afterwards he undertook his first defence of a prisoner on a capital charge, and secured by his eloquence the acquittal of Sextus Roscius on an accusation of having murdered his father. The charge appears to have been a mere conspiracy, wholly unsupported by evidence; but the accuser was a favourite with Sylla, whose power was all but absolute; and the innocence of the accused was a very insufficient protection before a Roman jury of those days. What kind of considerations, besides the merits of the case and the rhetoric of counsel, did usually sway these tribunals, we shall see hereafter. In consequence of this decided success, briefs came in upon the young pleader almost too quickly. Like many other successful orators, he had to combat some natural deficiencies; he had inherited from his father a somewhat delicate constitution; his lungs were not powerful, and his voice required careful management; and the loud declamation and vehement action which he had adopted from his models—and which were necessary conditions of success in the large arena in which a Roman advocate had to plead—he found very hard work. He left Rome for a while, and retired for rest and change to Athens.

The six months which he spent there, though busy and studious, must have been very pleasant ones. To one like Cicero, Athens was at once classic and holy ground. It combined all those associations and attractions which we might now expect to find in a visit to the capitals of Greece and of Italy, and a pilgrimage to Jerusalem. Poetry, rhetoric, philosophy, religion—all, to his eyes, had their cradle there. It was the home of all that was literature to him; and there, too, were the great Eleusinian mysteries—which are mysteries still, but which contained under their veil whatever faith in the Invisible and Eternal rested in the mind of an enlightened pagan. There can be little doubt but that Cicero took this opportunity of initiation. His brother Quintus and one of his cousins were with him at Athens; and in that city he also renewed his acquaintance with an old school-fellow, Titus Pomponius, who lived so long in the city, and became so thoroughly Athenian in his tastes and habits, that he is better known to us, as he was to his contemporaries, by the surname of Atticus, which was given him half in jest, than by his more sonorous Roman name. It is to the accidental circumstance of Atticus remaining so long a voluntary exile from Rome, and to the correspondence which was maintained between the two friends, with occasional intervals, for something like four-and-twenty years, that we are indebted for a more thorough insight into the character of Cicero than we have as to any other of the great minds of antiquity; nearly four hundred of his letters to Atticus, written in all the familiar confidence of private friendship by a man by no means reticent as to his personal feelings, having been preserved to us. Atticus's replies are lost; it is said that he was prudent enough, after his friend's unhappy death, to reclaim and destroy them. They would perhaps have told us, in his case, not very much that we care to know beyond what we know already. Rich, luxurious, with elegant tastes and easy morality—a true Epicurean, as he boasted himself to be—Atticus had nevertheless a kind heart and an open hand. He has generally been called selfish, somewhat unfairly; at least his selfishness never took the form of indifference or unkindness to others. In one sense he was a truer philosopher than Cicero: for he seems to have acted through life on that maxim of Socrates which his friend professed to approve, but certainly never followed, —that "a wise man kept out of public business". His vocation was certainly not patriotism; but the worldly wisdom which kept well with men of all political colours, and eschewed the wretched intrigues and bloody feuds of Rome, stands out in no unfavourable contrast with the conduct of many of her *soi-disant* patriots. If he declined to take a side himself, men of all parties resorted to him in their adversity; and the man who befriended the younger Marius in his exile, protected the widow of Antony, gave shelter on his estates to the victims of the triumvirate's proscription, and was always ready to offer his friend Cicero both his house and his purse whenever the political horizon clouded round him, —this man was surely as good a citizen as the noisiest clamourer for "liberty" in the Forum, or the readiest hand with the dagger. He kept his life and his property safe through all those years of peril and proscription, with less sacrifice of principle than many who had made louder professions, and died—by a singular act of voluntary starvation, to make short work with an incurable disease—at a ripe old age; a godless Epicurean, no doubt, but not the worst of them.

We must return to Cicero, and deal somewhat briefly with the next few years of his life. He extended his foreign tour for two years, visiting the chief cities of Asia Minor, remaining for a short time at Rhodes to take lessons once more from his old tutor Molo the rhetorician, and everywhere availing himself of the lectures of the most renowned Greek professors, to correct and improve his own style of composition and delivery. Soon after his return to Rome, he married. Of the character of his wife Terentia very different views have been taken. She appears to have written to him very kindly during his long forced absences. Her letters have not reached us; but in all her husband's replies she is mentioned in terms of apparently the most sincere affection. He calls her repeatedly his "darling"—"the delight of his eyes"—"the best of mothers; " yet he procured a divorce from her, for no distinctly assigned reason, after a married life of thirty years, during which we find no trace of any serious domestic unhappiness. The imputations on her honour made by Plutarch, and repeated by others, seem utterly without foundation; and Cicero's own share in the transaction is not improved by the fact of his taking another wife as soon as possible—a ward of his own, an almost girl, with whom he did not live a year before a second divorce released him. Terentia is said also to have had an imperious temper; but the only ground for this assertion seems to have been that she quarrelled occasionally with her sister-in-law Pomponia, sister of Atticus and wife of Quintus Cicero; and since Pomponia, by her own brother's account, showed her temper very disagreeably to her husband, the feud between the ladies was more likely to have been her fault than Terentia's. But the very low notion of the marriage relations entertained by both the later Greeks and Romans helps to throw some light upon a proceeding which would otherwise seem very mysterious. Terentia, as is pretty plain from the hints in her husband's letters, was not a good manager in money matters; there is room for suspicion that she was not even an honest one in his absence, and was "making a purse" for herself; she had thus failed in one of the only two qualifications which, according to Demosthenes—an authority who ranked very high in Cicero's eyes—were essential in a wife, to be "a faithful house-guardian" and "a fruitful mother". She did not die of a broken heart; she lived to be 104, and, according to Dio Cassius, to have three more husbands. Divorces were easy enough at Rome, and had the lady been a rich widow, there might be nothing so improbable in this latter part of the story, though she was fifty years old at the date of this first divorce. [1]

[Footnote 1: Cato, who is the favourite impersonation of all the moral virtues of his age, divorced his wife—to oblige a friend!]

CHAPTER II.

PUBLIC CAREER. — IMPEACHMENT OF VERRES.

Increasing reputation as a brilliant and successful pleader, and the social influence which this brought with it, secured the rapid succession of Cicero to the highest public offices. Soon after his marriage he was elected Quaestor—the first step on the official ladder—which, as he already possessed the necessary property qualification, gave him a seat in the Senate for life. The Aedileship and Praetorship followed subsequently, each as early, in point of age, as it could legally be held. [1] His practice as an advocate suffered no interruption, except that his Quaestorship involved his spending a year in Sicily. The Praetor who was appointed to the government of that province[2] had under him two quaestors, who were a kind of comptrollers of the exchequer; and Cicero was appointed to the western district, having his headquarters at Lilybaeum. In the administration of his office there he showed himself a thorough man of business. There was a dearth of corn at Rome that year, and Sicily was the great granary of the empire. The energetic measures which the new Quaestor took fully met the emergency. He was liberal to the tenants of the State, courteous and accessible to all, upright in his administration, and, above all, he kept his hands clean from bribes and peculation. The provincials were as much astonished as delighted: for Rome was not in the habit of sending them such officers. They invented honours for him such as had never been bestowed on any minister before.

[Footnote 1: The Quaestors (of whom there were at this time twenty) acted under the Senate as State treasurers. The Consul or other officer who commanded in chief during a campaign would be accompanied by one of them as paymaster-general.

The Aediles, who were four in number, had the care of all public buildings, markets, roads, and the State property generally. They had also the superintendence of the national festivals and public games.

The duties of the Praetors, of whom there were eight, were principally judicial. The two seniors, called the 'City' and 'Foreign' respectively, corresponded roughly to our Home and Foreign Secretaries. These were all gradual steps to the office of Consul.]

[Footnote 2: The provinces of Rome, in their relation to the mother-state of Italy, may be best compared with our own government of India, or such of our crown colonies as have no representative assembly. They had each their governor or lieutenant-governor, who must have been an ex-minister of Rome: a man who had been Consul went out with the rank of "pro-consul", —one who had been Praetor with the rank of "pro-praetor". These held office for one or two years, and had the power of life and death within their respective jurisdictions. They had under them one or more officers who bore the title of Quaestor, who collected the taxes and had the general management of the revenues of the province. The provinces at this time were Sicily, Sardinia with Corsica, Spain and Gaul (each in two divisions); Greece, divided into Macedonia and Achaia (the Morea); Asia, Syria, Cilicia, Bithynia, Cyprus, and Africa in four divisions. Others were added afterwards, under the Empire.]

No wonder the young official's head (he was not much over thirty) was somewhat turned. "I thought", he said, in one of his speeches afterwards—introducing with a quiet humour, and with all a practised orator's skill, one of those personal anecdotes which relieve a long speech—"I thought in my heart, at the time, that the people at Rome must be talking of nothing but my quaestorship". And he goes on to tell his audience how he was undeceived.

"The people of Sicily had devised for me unprecedented honours. So I left the island in a state of great elation, thinking that the Roman people would at once offer me everything without my seeking. But when I was leaving my province, and on my road home, I happened to land at Puteoli just at the time when a good many of our most fashionable people are accustomed to resort to that neighbourhood. I very nearly collapsed, gentlemen, when a man asked me what day I had left Rome, and whether there was any news stirring? When I made answer that I was returning from my province—'Oh! yes, to be sure', said he; 'Africa, I believe? ' 'No', said I to him, considerably annoyed and disgusted; 'from Sicily'. Then somebody else, with the air of a man who knew all about it, said to him—'What! don't you know that he was Quaestor at *Syracuse*? ' [It was at Lilybaeum—quite a different district.] No need to make a long story of it; I swallowed my indignation, and made as though I, like the rest, had come there for the waters. But I am not sure, gentlemen, whether that scene did not do me more good than if everybody then and there had publicly congratulated me. For after I had thus found out that the people of Rome have somewhat deaf ears, but very keen and sharp eyes, I left

off cogitating what people would hear about me; I took care that
thenceforth they should see me before them every day: I lived in
their sight, I stuck close to the Forum; the porter at my gate refused
no man admittance—my very sleep was never allowed to be a plea
against an audience". [1]

[Footnote 1: Defence of Plancius, c. 26, 27.]

Did we not say that Cicero was modern, not ancient? Have we not
here the original of that Cambridge senior wrangler, who, happening
to enter a London theatre at the same moment with the king, bowed
all round with a gratified embarrassment, thinking that the audience
rose and cheered at *him*?

It was while he held the office of Aedile that he made his first
appearance as public prosecutor, and brought to justice the most
important criminal of the day. Verres, late Praetor in Sicily, was
charged with high crimes and misdemeanours in his government.
The grand scale of his offences, and the absorbing interest of the trial,
have led to his case being quoted as an obvious parallel to that of
Warren Hastings, though with much injustice to the latter, so far as it
may seem to imply any comparison of moral character. This Verres,
the corrupt son of a corrupt father, had during his three years' rule
heaped on the unhappy province every evil which tyranny and
rapacity could inflict. He had found it prosperous and contented: he
left it exhausted and smarting under its wrongs. He met his
impeachment now with considerable confidence. The gains of his
first year of office were sufficient, he said, for himself; the second
had been for his friends; the third produced more than enough to
bribe a jury.

The trials at Rome took place in the Forum—the open space, of
nearly five acres, lying between the Capitoline and Palatine hills. It
was the city market-place, but it was also the place where the
population assembled for any public meeting, political or other—
where the idle citizen strolled to meet his friends and hear the gossip
of the day, and where the man of business made his appointments.
Courts for the administration of justice—magnificent halls, called
basilicae—had by this time been erected on the north and south sides,
and in these the ordinary trials took place; but for state trials the
open Forum was itself the court. One end of the wide area was
raised on a somewhat higher level—a kind of daïs on a large scale—
and was separated from the rest by the Rostra, a sort of stage from

which the orators spoke. It was here that the trials were held. A temporary tribunal for the presiding officer, with accommodation for counsel, witnesses, and jury, was erected in the open air; and the scene may perhaps best be pictured by imagining the principal square in some large town fitted up with open hustings on a large scale for an old-fashioned county election, by no means omitting the intense popular excitement and mob violence appropriate to such occasions. Temples of the gods and other public buildings overlooked the area, and the steps of these, on any occasion of great excitement, would be crowded by those who were anxious to see at least, if they could not hear.

Verres, as a state criminal, would be tried before a special commission, and by a jury composed at this time entirely from the senatorial order, chosen by lot (with a limited right of challenge reserved to both parties) from a panel made out every year by the praetor. This magistrate, who was a kind of minister of justice, usually presided on such occasions, occupying the curule chair, which was one of the well-known privileges of high office at Rome. But his office was rather that of the modern chairman who keeps order at a public meeting than that of a judge. Judge, in our sense of the word, there was none; the jury were the judges both of law and fact. They were, in short, the recognised assessors of the praetor, in whose hands the administration of justice was supposed to lie. The law, too, was of a highly flexible character, and the appeals of the advocates were rather to the passions and feelings of the jurors than to the legal points of the case. Cicero himself attached comparatively little weight to this branch of his profession; —"Busy as I am", he says in one of his speeches, "I could make myself lawyer enough in three days". The jurors gave each their vote by ballot, —'guilty', 'not guilty', or (as in the Scotch courts) 'not proven', —and the majority carried the verdict.

But such trials as that of Verres were much more like an impeachment before the House of Commons than a calm judicial inquiry. The men who would have to try a defendant of his class would be, in very few cases, honest and impartial weighers of the evidence. Their large number (varying from fifty to seventy) weakened the sense of individual responsibility, and laid them more open to the appeal of the advocates to their political passions. Most of them would come into court prejudiced in some degree by the interests of party; many would be hot partisans. Cicero, in his treatise on 'Oratory', explains clearly for the pleader's guidance the nature of the tribunals to which he had to appeal. "Men are influenced in their verdicts much more by prejudice or favour, or greed of gain, or anger, or indignation, or pleasure, or hope or fear, or by misapprehension, or by some excitement of their feelings, than either by the facts of the case, or by established precedents, or by any rules or principles whatever either of law or equity".

Verres was supported by some of the most powerful families at Rome. Peculation on the part of governors of provinces had become almost a recognised principle: many of those who held offices of state either had done, or were waiting their turn to do, much the same as the present defendant; and every effort had been made by his friends either to put off the trial indefinitely, or to turn it into a sham by procuring the appointment of a private friend and creature of his own as public prosecutor. On the other hand, the Sicilian families, whom he had wronged and outraged, had their share of influence also at Rome, and there was a growing impatience of the insolence and rapacity of the old governing houses, of whose worst qualities the ex-governor of Sicily was a fair type. There were many reasons which would lead Cicero to take up such a cause energetically. It was a great opening for him in what we may call his profession: his former connection with the government of Sicily gave him a personal interest in the cause of the province; and, above all, the prosecution of a state offender of such importance was a lift at once into the foremost ranks of political life. He spared no pains to get up his case thoroughly. He went all over the island collecting evidence; and his old popularity there did him good service in the work.

There was, indeed, evidence enough against the late governor. The reckless gratification of his avarice and his passions had seldom satisfied him, without the addition of some bitter insult to the sufferers. But there was even a more atrocious feature in the case, of which Cicero did not fail to make good use in his appeal to a Roman jury. Many of the unhappy victims had the Roman franchise. The torture of an unfortunate Sicilian might be turned into a jest by a clever advocate for the defence, and regarded by a philosophic jury with less than the cold compassion with which we regard the sufferings of the lower animals; but "to scourge a man that was a Roman and uncondemned", even in the far-off province of Judea, was a thought which, a century later, made the officers of the great Empire, at its pitch of power, tremble before a wandering teacher who bore the despised name of Christian. No one can possibly tell the tale so well as Cicero himself; and the passage from his speech for the prosecution is an admirable specimen both of his power of pathetic narrative and scathing denunciation, "How shall I speak of Publius Gavius, a citizen of Consa? With what powers of voice, with what force of language, with what sufficient indignation of soul, can I tell the tale? Indignation, at least, will not fail me: the more must I strive that in this my pleading the other requisites may be made to meet the gravity of the subject, the intensity of my feeling. For the accusation is such that, when it was first laid before me, I did not think to make use of it; though I knew it to be perfectly true, I did not think it would be credible. —How shall I now proceed? —when I have already been speaking for so many hours on one subject—his atrocious cruelty; when I have exhausted upon other points well-nigh all the powers of language such as alone is suited to that man's crimes; —when I have taken no precaution to secure your attention by any variety in my charges against him, —in what fashion can I now speak on a charge of this importance? I think there is one way— one course, and only one, left for me to take. I will place the facts before you; and they have in themselves such weight, that no eloquence—I will not say of mine, for I have none—but of any man's, is needed to excite your feelings.

"This Gavius of Consa, of whom I speak, had been among the crowds of Roman citizens who had been thrown into prison under that man. Somehow he had made his escape out of the Quarries, [1] and had got to Messana; and when he saw Italy and the towers of Rhegium now so close to him, and out of the horror and shadow of death felt himself breathe with a new life as he scented once more the fresh air of liberty and the laws, he began to talk at Messana, and to complain that he, a Roman citizen, had been put in irons—that he was going straight to Rome—that he would be ready there for Verres on his arrival.

[Footnote 1: This was one of the state prisons at Syracuse, so called, said to have been constructed by the tyrant Dionysius. They were the quarries from which the stone was dug for building the city, and had been converted to their present purpose. Cicero, who no doubt had seen the one in question, describes it as sunk to an immense depth in the solid rock. There was no roof; and the unhappy prisoners were exposed there "to the sun by day and to the rain and frosts by night". In these places the survivors of the unfortunate Athenian expedition against Syracuse were confined, and died in great numbers.]

"The wretched man little knew that he might as well have talked in this fashion in the governor's palace before his very face, as at Messana. For, as I told you before, this city he had selected for himself as the accomplice in his crimes, the receiver of his stolen goods, the confidant of all his wickedness. So Gavius is brought at once before the city magistrates; and, as it so chanced, on that very day Verres himself came to Messana. The case is reported to him; that there is a certain Roman citizen who complained of having been put into the Quarries at Syracuse; that as he was just going on board ship, and was uttering threats—really too atrocious—against Verres, they had detained him, and kept him in custody, that the governor himself might decide about him as should seem to him good. Verres thanks the gentlemen, and extols their goodwill and zeal for his interests. He himself, burning with rage and malice, comes down to the court. His eyes flashed fire; cruelty was written on every line of his face. All present watched anxiously to see to what lengths he meant to go, or what steps he would take; when suddenly he ordered the prisoner to be dragged forth, and to be stripped and bound in the open forum, and the rods to be got ready at once. The unhappy man cried out that he was a Roman citizen—that he had the municipal franchise of Consa—that he had served in a campaign with Lucius Pretius, a distinguished Roman knight, now engaged in business at Panormus, from whom Verres might ascertain the truth of his statement. Then that man replies that he has discovered that he, Gavius, has been sent into Sicily as a spy by the ringleaders of the runaway slaves; of which charge there was neither witness nor trace of any kind, or even suspicion in any man's mind. Then he ordered the man to be scourged severely all over his body. Yes—a Roman citizen was cut to pieces with rods in the open forum at Messana, gentlemen; and as the punishment went on, no word, no groan of the wretched man, in all his anguish, was heard amid the sound of the lashes, but this cry, —'I am a Roman citizen! ' By such protest of citizenship he thought he could at least save himself from anything like blows—could escape the indignity of personal torture. But not only did he fail in thus deprecating the insult of the lash, but when he redoubled his entreaties and his appeal to the name of Rome, a cross—yes, I say, a cross—was ordered for that most unfortunate and ill-fated man, who had never yet beheld such an abuse of a governor's power.

"O name of liberty, sweet to our ears! O rights of citizenship, in which we glory! O laws of Porcius and Sempronius! O privilege of the tribune, long and sorely regretted, and at last restored to the people of Rome! Has it all come to this, that a Roman citizen in a province of the Roman people—in a federal town—is to be bound and beaten with rods in the forum by a man who only holds those rods and axes—those awful emblems—by grace of that same people of Rome? What shall I say of the fact that fire, and red-hot plates, and other tortures were applied? Even if his agonised entreaties and pitiable cries did not check you, were you not moved by the tears and groans which burst from the Roman citizens who were present at the scene? Did you dare to drag to the cross any man who claimed to be a citizen of Rome? —I did not intend, gentlemen, in my former pleading, to press this case so strongly—I did not indeed; for you saw yourselves how the public feeling was already embittered against the defendant by indignation, and hate, and dread of a common peril".

He then proceeds to prove by witnesses the facts of the case and the falsehood of the charge against Gavius of having been a spy. "However", he goes on to say, addressing himself now to Verres, "we will grant, if you please, that your suspicions on this point, if false, were honestly entertained".

"You did not know who the man was; you suspected him of being a spy. I do not ask the grounds of your suspicion. I impeach you on your own evidence. He said he was a Roman citizen. Had you yourself, Verres, been seized and led out to execution, in Persia, say, or in the farthest Indies, what other cry or protest could you raise but that you were a Roman citizen? And if you, a stranger there among strangers, in the hands of barbarians, amongst men who dwell in the farthest and remotest regions of the earth, would have found protection in the name of your city, known and renowned in every nation under heaven, could the victim whom you were dragging to the cross, be he who he might—and you did not know who he was—when he declared he was a citizen of Rome, could he obtain from you, a Roman magistrate, by the mere mention and claim of citizenship, not only no reprieve, but not even a brief respite from death?

"Men of neither rank nor wealth, of humble birth and station, sail the seas; they touch at some spot they never saw before, where they are neither personally known to those whom they visit, nor can always find any to vouch for their nationality. But in this single fact of their citizenship they feel they shall be safe, not only with our own governors, who are held in check by the terror of the laws and of public opinion—not only among those who share that citizenship of Rome, and who are united with them by community of language, of laws, and of many things besides—but go where they may, this, they think, will be their safe guard. Take away this confidence, destroy this safeguard for our Roman citizens—once establish the principle that there is no protection in the words, 'I am a citizen of Rome'—that praetor or other magistrate may with impunity sentence to what punishment he will a man who says he is a Roman citizen, merely because somebody does not know it for a fact; and at once, by admitting such a defence, you are shutting up against our Roman citizens all our provinces, all foreign states, despotic or independent—all the whole world, in short, which has ever lain open to our national enterprise beyond all".

He turns again to Verres.

"But why talk of Gavius? as though it were Gavius on whom you were wreaking a private vengeance, instead of rather waging war against the very name and rights of Roman citizenship. You showed yourself an enemy, I say, not to the individual man, but to the common cause of liberty. For what meant it that, when the authorities of Messana, according to their usual custom, would have erected the cross behind their city on the Pompeian road, you ordered it to be set up on the side that looked toward the Strait? Nay, and added this—which you cannot deny, which you said openly in the hearing of all—that you chose that spot for this reason, that as he had called himself a Roman citizen, he might be able, from his cross of punishment, to see in the distance his country and his home! And so, gentlemen, that cross was the only one, since Messana was a city, that was ever erected on that spot. A point which commanded a view of Italy was chosen by the defendant for the express reason that the dying sufferer, in his last agony and torment, might see how the rights of the slave and the freeman were separated by that narrow streak of sea; that Italy might look upon a son of hers suffering the capital penalty reserved for slaves alone.

"It is a crime to put a citizen of Rome in bonds; it is an atrocity to scourge him; to put him to death is well-nigh parricide; what shall I say it is to crucify him? —Language has no word by which I may designate such an enormity. Yet with all this yon man was not content. 'Let him look', said he, 'towards his country; let him die in full sight of freedom and the laws'. It was not Gavius; it was not a single victim, unknown to fame, a mere individual Roman citizen; it was the common cause of liberty, the common rights of citizenship, which you there outraged and put to a shameful death".

But in order to judge of the thrilling effect of such passages upon a Roman jury, they must be read in the grand periods of the oration itself, to which no translation into a language so different in idiom and rhythm as English is from Latin can possibly do justice. The fruitless appeal made by the unhappy citizen to the outraged majesty of Rome, and the indignant demand for vengeance which the great orator founds upon it—proclaiming the recognised principle that, in every quarter of the world, the humblest wanderer who could say he was a Roman citizen should find protection in the name—will be always remembered as having supplied Lord Palmerston with one of his most telling illustrations. But this great speech of Cicero's—perhaps the most magnificent piece of declamation in any language—though written and preserved to us was never spoken. The whole of the pleadings in the case, which extend to some length, were composed for the occasion, no doubt, in substance, and we have to thank Cicero for publishing them afterwards in full. But Verres only waited to hear the brief opening speech of his prosecutor; he did not dare to challenge a verdict, but allowing judgment to go by default, withdrew to Marseilles soon after the trial opened. He lived there, undisturbed in the enjoyment of his plunder, long enough to see the fall and assassination of his great accuser, but only (as it is said) to share his fate soon afterwards as one of the victims of Antony's proscription. Of his guilt there can be no question; his fear to face a court in which he had many friends is sufficient presumptive evidence of it; but we must hesitate in assuming the deepness of its dye from the terrible invectives of Cicero. No sensible person will form an opinion upon the real merits of a case, even in an English court of justice now, entirely from the speech of the counsel for the prosecution. And if we were to go back a century or two, to the state trials of those days, we know that to form our estimate of a prisoner's guilt from such data only would be doing him a gross injustice. We have only to remember the exclamation of Warren Hastings himself, whose trial, as has been said, has so many points of resemblance with that of Verres, when Burke sat down after the torrent of eloquence which he had hurled against the accused in his opening speech for the prosecution; —"I thought myself for the moment", said Hastings, "the guiltiest man in England".

The result of this trial was to raise Cicero at once to the leadership—if so modern an expression may be used—of the Roman bar. Up to this time the position had been held by Hortensius, the counsel for Verres, whom Cicero himself calls "the king of the courts". He was eight years the senior of Cicero in age, and many more professionally, for he is said to have made his first public speech at nineteen. He had the advantage of the most extraordinary memory, a musical voice, and a rich flow of language: but Cicero more than implies that he was not above bribing a jury. It was not more disgraceful in those days than bribing a voter in our own. The two men were very unlike in one respect; Hortensius was a fop and an exquisite (he is said to have brought an action against a colleague for disarranging the folds of his gown), while Cicero's vanity was quite of another kind. After Verres's trial, the two advocates were frequently engaged together in the same cause and on the same side: but Hortensius seems quietly to have abdicated his forensic sovereignty before the rising fame of his younger rival. They became, ostensibly at least, personal friends. What jealousy there was between them, strange to say, seems always to have been on the side of Cicero, who could not be convinced of the friendly feeling which, on Hortensius's part, there seems no reason to doubt. After his rival's death, however, Cicero did full justice to his merits and his eloquence, and even inscribed to his memory a treatise on 'Glory', which has been lost.

CHAPTER III.

THE CONSULSHIP AND CATILINE.

There was no check as yet in Cicero's career. It had been a steady course of fame and success, honestly earned and well deserved; and it was soon to culminate in that great civil triumph which earned for him the proud title of *Pater Patriae*—the Father of his Country. It was a phrase which the orator himself had invented; and it is possible that, with all his natural self-complacency, he might have felt a little uncomfortable under the compliment, when he remembered on whom he had originally bestowed it—upon that Caius Marius, whose death in his bed at a good old age, after being seven times consul, he afterwards uses as an argument, in the mouth of one of his imaginary disputants, against the existence of an overruling Providence. In the prime of his manhood he reached the great object of a Roman's ambition—he became virtually Prime Minister of the republic: for he was elected, by acclamation rather than by vote, the first of the two consuls for the year, and his colleague, Caius Antonius (who had beaten the third candidate, the notorious Catiline, by a few votes only) was a man who valued his office chiefly for its opportunities of peculation, and whom Cicero knew how to manage. It is true that this high dignity—so jealous were the old republican principles of individual power—would last only for a year; but that year was to be a most eventful one, both for Cicero and for Rome. The terrible days of Marius and Sylla had passed, only to leave behind a taste for blood and licence amongst the corrupt aristocracy and turbulent commons. There were men amongst the younger nobles quite ready to risk their lives in the struggle for absolute power; and the mob was ready to follow whatever leader was bold enough to bid highest for their support.

It is impossible here to do much more than glance at the well-known story of Catiline's conspiracy. It was the attempt of an able and desperate man to make himself and his partisans masters of Rome by a bloody revolution. Catiline was a member of a noble but impoverished family, who had borne arms under Sylla, and had served an early apprenticeship in bloodshed under that unscrupulous leader. Cicero has described his character in terms which probably are not unfair, because the portrait was drawn by him, in the course of his defence of a young friend who had been too much connected with Catiline, for the distinct purpose of showing

the popular qualities which had dazzled and attracted so many of
the youth of Rome.

"He had about him very many of, I can hardly say the visible tokens,
but the adumbrations of the highest qualities. There was in his
character that which tempted him to indulge the worst passions, but
also that which spurred him to energy and hard work. Licentious
appetites burnt fiercely within him, but there was also a strong love
of active military service. I believe that there never lived on earth
such a monster of inconsistency, —such a compound of opposite
tastes and passions brought into conflict with each other. Who at one
time was a greater favourite with our most illustrious men? Who
was a closer intimate with our very basest? Who could be more
greedy of money than he was? Who could lavish it more profusely?
There were these marvellous qualities in the man, —he made friends
so universally, he retained them by his obliging ways, he was ready
to share what he had with them all, to help them at their need with
his money, his influence, his personal exertions—not stopping short
of the most audacious crime, if there was need of it. He could change
his very nature, and rule himself by circumstances, and turn and
bend in any direction. He lived soberly with the serious, he was a
boon companion with the gay; grave with the elders, merry with the
young; reckless among the desperate, profligate with the depraved.
With a nature so complex and many-sided, he not only collected
round him wicked and desperate characters from all quarters of the
world, but he also attracted many brave and good men by his
simulation of virtue. It would have been impossible for him to have
organised that atrocious attack upon the Commonwealth, unless that
fierce outgrowth of depraved passions had rested on some under-
stratum of agreeable qualities and powers of endurance".

Born in the same year with Cicero, his unsuccessful rival for the
consulship, and hating him with the implacable hatred with which a
bad, ambitious, and able man hates an opponent who is his superior
in ability and popularity as well as character, Catiline seems to have
felt, as his revolutionary plot ripened, that between the new consul
and himself the fates of Rome must choose. He had gathered round
him a band of profligate young nobles, deep in debt like himself, and
of needy and unscrupulous adventurers of all classes. He had
partisans who were collecting and drilling troops for him in several
parts of Italy. The programme was assassination, abolition of debts,
confiscation of property: so little of novelty is there in revolutionary
principles. The first plan had been to murder the consuls of the year

before, and seize the government. It had failed through his own impatience. He now hired assassins against Cicero, choosing the opportunity of the election of the incoming consuls, which always took place some time before their entrance on office. But the plot was discovered, and the election was put off. When it did take place, Cicero appeared in the meeting, wearing somewhat ostentatiously a corslet of bright steel, to show that he knew his danger; and Catiline's partisans found the place of meeting already occupied by a strong force of the younger citizens of the middle class, who had armed themselves for the consul's protection. The election passed off quietly, and Catiline was again rejected. A second time he tried assassination, and it failed—so watchful and well informed was the intended victim. And now Cicero, perhaps, was roused to a consciousness that one or other must fall; for in the unusually determined measures which he took in the suppression of the conspiracy, the mixture of personal alarm with patriotic indignation is very perceptible. By a fortunate chance, the whole plan of the conspirators was betrayed. Rebel camps had been formed not only in Italy, but in Spain and Mauritania: Rome was to be set on fire, the slaves to be armed, criminals let loose, the friends of order to be put out of the way. The consul called a meeting of the senate in the temple of Jupiter Stator, a strong position on the Palatine Hill, and denounced the plot in all its details, naming even the very day fixed for the outbreak. The arch-conspirator had the audacity to be present, and Cicero addressed him personally in the eloquent invective which has come to us as his "First Oration against Catiline". His object was to drive his enemy from the city to the camp of his partisans, and thus to bring matters at once to a crisis for which he now felt himself prepared. This daily state of public insecurity and personal danger had lasted too long, he said:

"Therefore, let these conspirators at once take their side; let them separate themselves from honest citizens, and gather themselves together somewhere else; let them put a wall between us, as I have often said. Let us have them no longer thus plotting the assassination of a consul in his own house, overawing our courts of justice with armed bands, besieging the senate-house with drawn swords, collecting their incendiary stores to burn our city. Let us at last be able to read plainly in every Roman's face whether he be loyal to his country or no. I may promise you this, gentlemen of the Senate— there shall be no lack of diligence on the part of your consuls; there will be, I trust, no lack of dignity and firmness on your own, of spirit amongst the Roman knights, of unanimity amongst all honest men, but that when Catiline has once gone from us, everything will be not only discovered and brought into the light of day, but also crushed, —ay, and punished. Under such auspices, I bid you, Catiline. go forth to wage your impious and unhallowed war. —go, to the salvation of the state, to your own overthrow and destruction, to the ruin of all who have joined you in your great wickedness and treason. And thou, great Jupiter, whose worship Romulus founded here coeval with our city; —whom we call truly the 'Stay'[1] of our capital and our empire; thou wilt protect thine own altars and the temples of thy kindred gods, the walls and roof-trees of our homes, the lives and fortunes of our citizens, from yon man and his accomplices. These enemies of all good men, invaders of their country, plunderers of Italy, linked together in a mutual bond of crime and an alliance of villany, thou wilt surely, visit with an everlasting punishment, living and dead'".

[Footnote 1: 'Stator'.]

Catiline's courage did not fail him. He had been sitting alone—for, all the other senators had shrunk away from the bench of which he had taken possession. He rose, and in reply to Cicero, in a forced tone of humility protested his innocence. He tried also another point. Was he, —a man of ancient and noble family; —to be hastily condemned by his fellow-nobles on the word of this 'foreigner', as he contemptuously called Cicero—this *parvenu* from Arpinum? But the appeal failed; his voice was drowned in the cries of 'traitor' which arose on all sides, and with threats and curses, vowing that since he was driven to desperation he would involve all Rome in his ruin, he rushed out of the Senate-house. At dead of night he left the city, and joined the insurgent camp at Faesulae.

When the thunders of Cicero's eloquence had driven Catiline from the Senate-house, and forced him to join his fellow-traitors, and so put himself in the position of levying open war against the state, it remained to deal with those influential conspirators who had been detected and seized within the city walls. In three subsequent speeches in the Senate he justified the course he had taken in allowing Catiline to escape, exposed further particulars of the conspiracy, and urged the adoption of strong measures to crush it out within the city. Even now, not all Cicero's eloquence, nor all the efforts of our imagination to realise, as men realised it then, the imminence of the public danger, can reconcile the summary process adopted by the consul with our English notions of calm and deliberate justice. Of the guilt of the men there was no doubt; most of them even admitted it. But there was no formal trial; and a few hours after a vote of death had been passed upon them in a hesitating Senate, Lentulus and Cethegus, two members of that august body, with three of their companions in guilt, were brought from their separate places of confinement, with some degree of secrecy (as appears from different writers), carried down into the gloomy prison-vaults of the Tullianum, [1] and there quietly strangled, by the sole authority of the consul. Unquestionably they deserved death, if ever political criminals deserved it: the lives and liberties of good citizens were in danger; it was necessary to strike deep and strike swiftly at a conspiracy which extended no man knew how widely, and in which men like Julius Caesar and Crassus were strongly suspected of being engaged. The consuls had been armed with extra-constitutional powers, conveyed by special resolution of the Senate in the comprehensive formula that they "were to look to it that the state suffered no damage". Still, without going so far as to call this unexampled proceeding, as the German critic Mommsen does, "an act of the most brutal tyranny", it is easy to understand how Mr. Forsyth, bringing a calm and dispassionate legal judgment to bear upon the case, finds it impossible to reconcile it with our ideas of dignified and even-handed justice. [2] It was the hasty instinct of self-preservation, the act of a weak government uncertain of its very friends, under the influence of terror—a terror for which, no doubt, there were abundant grounds. When Cicero stood on the prison steps, where he had waited to receive the report of those who were making sure work with the prisoners within, and announced their fate to the assembled crowd below in the single word "*Vixerunt*" (a euphemism which we can only weakly translate into "They have lived their life"), no doubt he felt that he and the republic held theirs from that moment by a firmer tenure; no doubt very many of those who heard him felt that they could breathe again, now that the grasp of Catiline's assassins was, for the moment at all events, off their throats; and the crowd who followed the consul home were sincere enough when they hailed such a vigorous avenger as the 'Father of his Country'. But none the less it was that which politicians have called worse than a crime—it was a political blunder; and Cicero came to find it so in after years; though—partly from his immense self-appreciation, and partly from an honest determination to stand by his act and deed in all its consequences— he never suffered the shadow of such a confession to appear in his most intimate correspondence. He claimed for himself ever afterwards the sole glory of having saved the state by such prompt and decided action; and in this he was fully borne out by the facts: justifiable or unjustifiable, the act was his; and there were burning hearts at Rome which dared not speak out against the popular consul, but set it down to his sole account against the day of retribution.

[Footnote 1: A state dungeon, said to have been built in the reign of Servius Tullius. It was twelve feet under ground. Executions often took place there, and the bodies of the criminals were afterwards thrown down the Gemonian steps (which were close at hand) into the Forum, for the people to see.]

[Footnote 2: Life of Cicero, p. 119.]

For the present, however, all went successfully. The boldness of the consul's measures cowed the disaffected, and confirmed the timid and wavering. His colleague Antonius—himself by no means to be depended on at this crisis, having but lately formed a coalition with Catiline as against Cicero in the election for consuls—had, by judicious management, been got away from Rome to take the command against the rebel army in Etruria. He did not, indeed, engage in the campaign actively in person, having just now a fit of the gout, either real or pretended; but his lieutenant-general was an old soldier who cared chiefly for his duty, and Catiline's band— reckless and desperate men who had gathered to his camp from all motives and from all quarters—were at length brought to bay, and died fighting hard to the last. Scarcely a man of them, except the slaves and robbers who had swelled their ranks, either escaped or was made prisoner. Catiline's body—easily recognised by his remarkable height—was found, still breathing, lying far in advance of his followers, surrounded by the dead bodies of the Roman legionaries—for the loss on the side of the Republic had been very severe. The last that remained to him of the many noble qualities which had marked his earlier years was a desperate personal courage.

For the month that yet remained of his consulship, Cicero was the foremost man in Rome—and, as a consequence, in the whole world. Nobles and commons vied in doing honour to the saviour of the state. Catulus and Cato—men from whose lips words of honour came with a double weight—saluted him publicly by that memorable title of *Pater Patriae*; and not only the capital, but most of the provincial towns of Italy, voted him some public testimony of his unrivalled services. No man had a more profound appreciation of those services than the great orator himself. It is possible that other men have felt quite as vain of their own exploits, and on far less grounds; but surely no man ever paraded his self-complacency like Cicero. His vanity was indeed a thing to marvel at rather than to smile at, because it was the vanity of so able a man. Other great men have been either too really great to entertain the feeling, or have been wise enough to keep it to themselves. But to Cicero it must have been one of the enjoyments of his life. He harped upon his consulship in season and out of season, in his letters, in his judicial pleadings, in his public speeches (and we may be sure in his conversation), until one would think his friends must have hated the subject even more than his enemies. He wrote accounts of it in prose and verse, in Latin and Greek—and, no doubt, only limited them to those languages because they were the only ones he knew. The well-known line which provoked the ridicule of critics like Juvenal and Quintilian, because of the unlucky jingle peculiarly unpleasant to a Roman ear:

"O fortunatam natam me consule Romam! "

expresses the sentiment which—rhyme or no rhyme, reason or no reason—he was continually repeating in some form or other to himself and to every one who would listen.

His consulship closed in glory; but on his very last day of office there was a warning voice raised amidst the triumph, which might have opened his eyes—perhaps it did—to the troubles which were to come. He stood up in the Rostra to make the usual address to the people on laying down his authority. Metellus Nepos had been newly elected one of the tribunes: it was his office to guard jealously all the rights and privileges of the Roman commons. Influenced, it is said, by Caesar—possibly himself an undiscovered partisan of Catiline—he dealt a blow at the retiring consul under cover of a discharge of duty. As Cicero was about to speak, he interposed a tribune's 'veto'; no man should be heard, he said, who *had put Roman citizens to death without a trial*. There was consternation in the Forum. Cicero could not dispute what was a perfectly legal exercise of the tribune's power; only, in a few emphatic words which he seized the opportunity of adding to the usual formal oath on quitting office, he protested that his act had saved Rome. The people shouted in answer, "Thou hast said true! " and Cicero went home a private citizen, but with that hearty tribute from his grateful countrymen ringing pleasantly in his ears. But the bitter words of Metellus were yet to be echoed by his enemies again and again, until that fickle popular voice took them up, and howled them after the once popular consul.

Let us follow him for a while into private life; a pleasanter companionship for us, we confess, than the unstable glories of the political arena at Rome. In his family and social relations, the great orator wins from us an amount of personal interest and sympathy which he fails sometimes to command in his career as a statesman. At forty-five years of age he has become a very wealthy man—has bought for something like £30,000 a noble mansion on the Palatine Hill; and besides the old-fashioned family seat near Arpinum—now become his own by his father's death—he has built, or enlarged, or bought as they stood, villas at Antium, at Formiae, at Pompeii, at Cumae, at Puteoli, and at half-a-dozen other places, besides the one favourite spot of all, which was to him almost what Abbotsford was to Scott, the home which it was the delight of his life to embellish— his country-house among the pleasant hills of Tusculum. [1] It had once belonged to Sulla, and was about twelve miles from Rome. In that beloved building and its arrangements he indulged, as an ample purse allowed him, not only a highly-cultivated taste, but in some respects almost a whimsical fancy. "A mere cottage", he himself terms it in one place; but this was when he was deprecating accusations of extravagance which were brought against him, and we all understand something of the pride which in such matters "apes humility". He would have it on the plan of the Academia at Athens, with its *palaestra* and open colonnade, where, as he tells us, he could walk and discuss politics or philosophy with his friends. Greek taste and design were as fashionable among the Romans of that day as the Louis Quatorze style was with our grandfathers. But its grand feature was a library, and its most valued furniture was books. Without books, he said, a house was but a body without a soul. He entertained for these treasures not only the calm love of a reader, but the passion of a bibliophile; he was particular about his bindings, and admired the gay colours of the covers in which the precious manuscripts were kept as well as the more intellectual beauties within. He had clever Greek slaves employed from time to time in making copies of all such works as were not to be readily purchased. He could walk across, too, as he tells us, to his neighbour's, the young Lucullus, a kind of ward of his, and borrow from the library of that splendid mansion any book he wanted. His friend Atticus collected for him everywhere—manuscripts, paintings, statuary; though for sculpture he professes not to care much, except for such subjects as might form appropriate decorations for his *palaestra* and his library. Very pleasant must have been the days spent together by the two friends—so alike in their private tastes and habits, so far apart in their chosen course of life—when they met there in the brief holidays which Cicero stole from the law-courts and the Forum, and sauntered in the shady walks, or lounged in the cool library, in that home of lettered ease, where the busy lawyer and politician declared that he forgot for a while all the toils and vexations of public life.

[Footnote 1: Near the modern town of Frascati. But there is no certainty as to the site of Cicero's villa.]

He had his little annoyances, however, even in these happy hours of retirement. Morning calls were an infliction to which a country gentleman was liable in ancient Italy as in modern England. A man like Cicero was very good company, and somewhat of a lion besides; and country neighbours, wherever he set up his rest, insisted on bestowing their tediousness on him. His villa at Formiae, his favourite residence next to Tusculum, was, he protested, more like a public hall. Most of his visitors, indeed, had the consideration not to trouble him after ten or eleven in the forenoon (fashionable calls in those days began uncomfortably early); but there were one or two, especially his next-door neighbour, Arrius, and a friend's friend, named Sebosus, who were in and out at all hours: the former had an unfortunate taste for philosophical discussion, and was postponing his return to Rome (he was good enough to say) from day to day in order to enjoy these long mornings in Cicero's conversation. Such are the doleful complaints in two or three of the letters to Atticus; but, like all such complaints, they were probably only half in earnest: popularity, even at a watering-place, was not very unpleasant, and the writer doubtless knew how to practise the social philosophy which he recommends to others, and took his place cheerfully and pleasantly in the society which he found about him—not despising his honest neighbours because they had not all adorned a consulship or saved a state.

There were times when Cicero fancied that this rural life, with all its refinements of wealth and taste and literary leisure, was better worth living than the public life of the capital. His friends and his books, he said, were the company most congenial to him; "politics might go to the dogs; " to count the waves as they rolled on the beach was happiness; he "had rather be mayor of Antium than consul at Rome"; "rather sit in his own library with Atticus in their favourite seat under the bust of Aristotle than in the curule chair". It is true that these longings for retirement usually followed some political defeat or mortification; that his natural sphere, the only life in which he could be really happy, was in the keen excitement of party warfare—the glorious battle-field of the Senate and the Forum. The true key-note of his mind is to be found in these words to his friend Coelius: "Cling to the city, my friend, and live in her light: all employment abroad, as I have felt from my earliest manhood, is obscure and petty for those who have abilities to make them famous at Rome". Yet the other strain had nothing in it of affectation, or hypocrisy: it was the schoolboy escaped from work, thoroughly enjoying his holiday, and fancying that nothing would be so delightful as to have holidays always. In this, again, there was a similarity between Cicero's taste and that of Horace. The poet loved his Sabine farm and all its rural delights—after his fashion; and perhaps thought honestly that he loved it more than he really did. Above all, he loved to write about it. With that fancy, half-real, perhaps, and half-affected, for pastoral simplicity, which has always marked a state of over-luxurious civilisation, he protests to himself that there is nothing like the country. But perhaps Horace discharges a sly jest at himself, in a sort of aside to his readers, in the person of Alphius, the rich city money-lender, who is made to utter that pretty apostrophe to rural happiness:

> "Happy the man, in busy schemes unskilled,
> Who, living simply, like our sires of old,
> Tills the few acres which his father tilled,
> Vexed by no thoughts of usury or gold".
> Martin's 'Horace'

And who, after thus expatiating for some stanzas on the charms of the country, calls in all his money one week in order to settle there, and puts it all out again (no doubt at higher interest) the week after. "*O rus, quando to aspiciam!* " has been the cry of public men before and since Cicero's day, to whom, as to the great Roman, banishment from political life, and condemnation to perpetual leisure, would have been a sentence that would have crushed their very souls.

He was very happy at this time in his family. His wife and he loved one another with an honest affection; anything more would have been out of the natural course of things in Roman society at any date, and even so much as this was become a notable exception in these later days. It is paying a high honour to the character of Cicero and his household—and from all evidence that has come down to us it may be paid with truth—that even in those evil times it might have presented the original of what Virgil drew as almost a fancy picture, or one to be realised only in some happy retirement into which the civilised vices of the capital had never penetrated—

> "Where loving children climb to reach a kiss—
> A home of chaste delights and wedded bliss. [1]"

His little daughter, Tullia, or Tulliola, which was her pet name (the Roman diminutives being formed somewhat more elegantly than ours, by adding a syllable instead of cutting short), was the delight of his heart in his earlier letters to Atticus he is constantly making some affectionate mention of her—sending her love, or some playful message which his friend would understand. She had been happily married (though she was then but thirteen at the most) the year before his consulship; but the affectionate intercourse between father and daughter was never interrupted until her early death. His only son, Marcus, born after a considerable interval, who succeeded to Tullia's place as a household pet, is made also occasionally to send some childish word of remembrance to his father's old friend:

"Cicero the Little sends his compliments to Titus the Athenian"—"Cicero the Philosopher salutes Titus the Politician. [2]" These messages are written in Greek at the end of the letters. Abeken thinks that in the originals they might have been added in the little Cicero's own hand, "to show that he had begun Greek; " "a conjecture", says Mr. Merivale, "too pleasant not to be readily admitted". The boy gave his father some trouble in after life. He served with some credit as an officer of cavalry under Pompey in Greece, or at least got into no trouble there. Some years after, he wished to take service in Spain, under Caesar, against the sons of Pompey; but the father did not approve of this change of side. He persuaded him to go to Athens to study instead, allowing him what both Atticus and himself thought a very liberal income—not sufficient, however, for him to keep a horse, which Cicero held to be an unnecessary luxury. Probably the young cavalry officer might not have been of the same opinion; at any rate, he got into more trouble among the philosophers than he did in the army. He spent a great deal more than his allowance, and one of the professors, whose lectures he attended, had the credit of helping him to spend it. The young man must have shared the kindly disposition of his father. He wrote a confidential letter to Tiro, the old family servant, showing very good feeling, and promising reformation. It is doubtful how far the promise was kept. He rose, however, subsequently to place and power under Augustus, but died without issue; and, so far at least as history knows them, the line of the Ciceros was extinct. It had flashed into fame with the great orator, and died out with him.

[Footnote 1: "Interia dulces pendent circum oscula nati; Casta pudicitiam servat domus". —Georg. ii. 524.]

[Footnote 2: See 'Letters to Atticus', ii. 9, 12; Merivale's translation of Abeken's 'Cicero in Seinen Briefen', p. 114.]

All Cicero's biographers have found considerable difficulty in tracing, at all satisfactorily, the sources of the magnificent fortune which must have been required to keep up, and to embellish in accordance with so luxurious a taste, so many residences in all parts of the country. True, these expenses often led Cicero into debt and difficulties; but what he borrowed from his friends he seems always to have repaid, so that the money must have come in from some quarter or other. His patrimony at Arpinum would not appear to have been large; he got only some £3000 or £4000 dowry with Terentia; and we find no hint of his making money by any commercial speculations, as some Roman gentlemen did. On the other hand, it is the barest justice to him to say that his hands were clean from those ill-gotten gains which made the fortunes of many of the wealthiest public men at Rome, who were criminals in only a less degree than Verres—peculation, extortion, and downright robbery in the unfortunate provinces which they were sent out to govern. Such opportunities lay as ready to his grasp as to other men's, but he steadily eschewed them. His declining the tempting prize of a provincial government, which was his right on the expiration of his praetorship, may fairly be attributed to his having in view the higher object of the consulship, to secure which, by an early and persistent canvass, he felt it necessary to remain in Rome. But he again waived the right when his consulship was over; and when, some years afterwards, he went unwillingly as pro-consul to Cilicia, his administration there, as before in his lower office in Sicily, was marked by a probity and honesty quite exceptional in a Roman governor. His emoluments, confined strictly within the legal bounds, would be only moderate, and, whatever they were, came too late in his life to be any explanation of his earlier expenditure. He received many valuable legacies, at different times, from personal friends or grateful clients who died childless (be it remembered how the barrenness of the marriage union had become then, at Rome, as it is said to be in some countries now, the reproach of a sensual and effete aristocracy); he boasts himself, in one of his 'Philippics', that he had received from this source above £170,000. Mr. Forsyth also notices the large presents that were made by foreign kings and states to conciliate the support and advocacy of the leading men at Rome— "we can hardly call them bribes, for in many cases the relation of patron and client was avowedly established between a foreign state and some influential Roman: and it became his duty, as of course it was his interest, to defend it in the Senate and before the people". In this way, he thinks, Cicero held "retainers" from Dyrrachium; and, he might have added, from Sicily. The great orator's own boast was, that he never took anything for his services as an advocate; and, indeed, such payments were forbidden by law. [1] But with all respect for Cicero's material honesty, one learns from his letters, unfortunately, not to put implicit confidence in him when he is in a boasting vein; and he might not look upon voluntary gifts, after a cause was decided, in the light of payment. Paetus, one of his clients, gave him a valuable library of books; and one cannot believe that this was a solitary instance of the quiet evasion of the Cincian law, or that there were not other transactions of the same nature which never found their way into any letter of Cicero's that was likely to come down to us.

[Footnote 1: The principle passed, like so many others, from the old Roman law into our own, so that to this very day, a barrister's fees, being considered in the nature of an *honorarium*, or voluntary present made to him for his services, are not recoverable by law.]

CHAPTER IV.

HIS EXILE AND RETURN.

We must return to Rome. Cicero had never left it but for his short occasional holiday. Though no longer in office, the ex-consul was still one of the foremost public men, and his late dignity gave him important precedence in the Senate. He was soon to be brought into contact, and more or less into opposition, with the two great chiefs of parties in whose feuds he became at length so fatally involved. Pompey and Caesar were both gradually becoming formidable, and both had ambitious plans of their own, totally inconsistent with any remnant of republican liberty—plans which Cicero more or less suspected, and of that suspicion they were probably both aware. Both, by their successful campaigns, had not only acquired fame and honours, but a far more dangerous influence—an influence which was to overwhelm all others hereafter—in the affection of their legions. Pompey was still absent in Spain, but soon to return from his long war against Mithridates, to enjoy the most splendid triumph ever seen at Rome, and to take the lead of the oligarchical party just so long and so far as they would help him to the power he coveted. The enemies whom Cicero had made by his strong measures in the matter of the Catilinarian conspiracy now took advantage of Pompey's name and popularity to make an attack upon him. The tribune Metellus, constant to his old party watchword, moved in the Senate that the successful general, upon whom all expectations were centred, should be recalled to Rome with his army "to restore the violated constitution". All knew against whom the motion was aimed, and what the violation of the constitution meant; it was the putting citizens to death without a trial. The measure was not passed, though Caesar, jealous of Cicero even more than of Pompey, lent himself to the attempt.

But the blow fell on Cicero at last from a very different quarter, and from the mere private grudge of a determined and unprincipled man. Publius Clodius, a young man of noble family, once a friend and supporter of Cicero against Catiline, but who had already made himself notorious for the most abandoned profligacy, was detected, in a woman's dress, at the celebration of the rites of the Bona Dea—a kind of religious freemasonry amongst the Roman ladies, the mysteries of which are very little known, and probably would in any case be best left without explanation. But for a man to have been present at them was a sacrilege hitherto unheard of, and which was held to lay the whole city under the just wrath of the offended goddess. The celebration had been held in the house of Caesar, as praetor, under the presidency of his wife Pompeia; and it was said that the object of the young profligate was an intrigue with that lady. The circumstances are not favourable to the suspicion; but Caesar divorced her forthwith, with the often-quoted remark that "Caesar's wife must not be even suspected". For this crime—unpardonable even in that corrupt society, when crimes of far deeper dye passed almost unreproved—Clodius was, after some delay, brought to public trial. The defence set up was an *alibi*, and Cicero came forward as a witness to disprove it: he had met and spoken with Clodius in Rome that very evening. The evidence was clear enough, but the jury had been tampered with by Clodius and his friends; liberal bribery, and other corrupting influences of even a more disgraceful kind, had been successfully brought to bear upon the majority of them, and he escaped conviction by a few votes. But he never forgave the part which Cicero had taken against him; and from that time forth the latter found a new, unscrupulous, indefatigable enemy, of whose services his old opponents gladly availed themselves. Cicero himself for some time underrated this new danger. He lost no opportunity of taunting the unconvicted criminal in the bitterest terms in the Senate, and of exchanging with him— very much to the detriment of his own character and dignity, in our modern eyes—the coarsest jests when they met in the street. But the temptation to a jest, of whatever kind, was always irresistible to Cicero: it was a weakness for which he more than once paid dearly, for they were remembered against him when be had forgotten them. Meanwhile Clodius—a sort of milder Catiline, not without many popular qualities—had got himself elected tribune; degrading himself formally from his own order of nobles for that purpose, since the tribune must be a man of the commons. The powers of the office were formidable for all purposes of obstruction and attack; Clodius had taken pains to ingratiate himself with all classes; and the consuls of the year were men of infamous character, for whom he had, found a successful means of bribery by the promise of getting a special law passed to secure them the choice of the richest provincial governments—those coveted fields of plunder—of which they would otherwise have had to take their chance by lot. When all was ripe for his revenge, he brought before the people in full assembly the following bill of pains and penalties: —"Be it enacted, that whoever has put to death a Roman citizen uncondemned in due form of trial, shall be interdicted from fire and water". Such was the legal form of words which implied banishment from Rome, outlawry, and social excommunication. Every man knew against whom the motion was levelled. It was carried—carried in spite of the indignation of all honest men in Rome, in spite of all Cicero's humiliating efforts to obtain its rejection.

It was in vain that he put on mourning, as was the custom with those who were impeached of public crimes, and went about the streets thus silently imploring the pity of his fellow-citizens. In vain the whole of his own equestrian order, and in fact, as he declares, "all honest men" (it was his favourite term for men of his own party); adopted the same dress to show their sympathy, and twenty thousand youths of good family—all in mourning—accompanied him through the city. The Senate even met and passed a resolution that their whole house should put on mourning too. But Gabinius, one of the consuls, at once called a public meeting, and warned the people not to make the mistake of thinking that the Senate was Rome.

In vain, also, was any personal appeal which Cicero could make to the only two men who might have had influence enough to sway the popular vote. He was ostensibly on good terms both with Pompey and Caesar; in fact, he made it his policy so to be. He foresaw that on their future course would probably depend the fate of Rome, and he persuaded himself, perhaps honestly, that he could make them "better citizens". But he trusted neither; and both saw in him an obstacle to their own ambition. Caesar now looked on coldly, not altogether sorry at the turn which affairs had taken, and faintly suggested that perhaps some "milder measure" might serve to meet the case. From Pompey Cicero had a right to look for some active support; indeed, such had been promised in case of need. He threw himself at his feet with prayers and tears, but even this last humiliation was in vain; and he anticipated the execution of that disgraceful edict by a voluntary withdrawal into exile. Piso, one of the consuls, had satirically suggested that thus he might "save Rome" a second time. His property was at once confiscated; his villas at Tusculum and at Formiae were plundered and laid waste, the consuls claiming the lion's share of the spoil; and Clodius, with his armed mob, set fire to the noble house on the Palatine, razed it to the ground, and erected on the site a temple to—*Liberty*!

Cicero had friends who strongly urged him to defy the edict; to remain at Rome, and call on all good citizens to arm in his defence.

Modern historians very generally have assumed that, if he could have made up his mind to such a course, it would probably have been successful. He was to rely, we suppose, upon those "twenty thousand Roman youths "—rather a broken reed to trust to (remembering what those young gallants were), with Caesar against him, now at the head of his legions just outside the gates of Rome. He himself seriously contemplated suicide, and consulted his friends as to the propriety of such a step in the gravest and most business-like manner; though, with our modern notions on the subject, such a consultation has more of the ludicrous than the sublime. The sensible and practical Atticus convinced him that such a solution of his difficulties would be the greatest possible mistake—a mistake, moreover, which could never be rectified.

But almost any course would have become him better than that which he chose. Had he remained and faced Clodius and his bravos manfully—or had he turned his back upon Rome for ever, and shaken the dust off his feet against the ungrateful city, and become a noble pensioner upon Atticus at Buthrotum—he would have died a greater man. He wandered from place to place sheltered by friends whose unselfish loyalty marks their names with honour in that false and evil generation—Sica, and Flaccus, and Plancius—bemoaning himself like a woman, —"too blinded with tears to write", "loathing the light of day". Atticus thought he was going mad. It is not pleasant to dwell upon this miserable weakness of a great mind, which Cicero's most eager eulogists admit, and which his detractors have not failed to make the most of. Nor is it easy to find excuse for him, but we will give him all the benefit of Mr. Forsyth's defence:

"Seldom has misfortune so crushed a noble spirit, and never, perhaps, has the 'bitter bread of banishment' seemed more bitter to any one than to him. We must remember that the love of country was a passion with the ancients to a degree which it is now difficult to realise, and exile from it even for a time was felt to be an intolerable evil. The nearest approach to such a feeling was perhaps that of some favourite under an European monarchy, when, frowned upon by his sovereign, he was hurled from place and power, and banished from the court. The change to Cicero was indeed tremendous. Not only was he an exile from Rome, the scene of all his hopes, his glories, his triumphs, but he was under the ban of an outlaw. If found within a certain distance from the capital, he must die, and it was death to any one to give him food or shelter. His property was destroyed, his family was penniless, and the people whom he had so faithfully served were the authors of his ruin. All this may be urged in his behalf, but still it would have been only consistent with Roman fortitude to have shown that he possessed something of the spirit of the fallen archangel". [1]

[Footnote 1: Forsyth's Life of Cicero, p. 190.]

His exile lasted nearly a year and a half. Long before that time there had come a reaction in his favour. The new consuls were well disposed towards him; Clodius's insolence had already disgusted Pompey; Caesar was absent with his legions in Gaul; his own friends, who had all along been active in his favour (though in his querulous mood he accused them of apathy) took advantage of the change, his generous rival Hortensius being amongst the most active; and all the frantic violence of Clodius and his party served only to delay for a while the return which they could not prevent. A motion for his recall was carried at last by an immense majority.

Cicero had one remarkable ally on that occasion. On one of the days when the Senate was known to be discussing his recall, the 'Andromache' of Ennius was being played in the theatre. The popular actor Esop, whose name has come down to us in conjunction with that of Roscius, was playing the principal character. The great orator had been his pupil, and was evidently regarded by him as a personal friend. With all the force of his consummate art, he threw into Andromache's lament for her absent father his own feelings for Cicero. The words in the part were strikingly appropriate, and he did not hesitate to insert a phrase or two of his own when he came to speak of the man

> "Who with a constant mind upheld the state,
> Stood on the people's side in perilous times,
> Ne'er reeked of his own life, nor spared himself".

So significant and empathetic were his tone and gesture as he addressed himself pointedly to his Roman audience, that they recalled him, and, amid a storm of plaudits, made him repeat the passage. He added to it the words—which were not set down for him—

> "Best of all friends in direst strait of war! "

and the applause was redoubled. The actor drew courage from his success. When, as the play went on, he came to speak the words—

"And you—you let him live a banished man—
See him driven forth and hunted from your gates! "

he pointed to the nobles, knights, and commons, as they sat in their respective seats in the crowded rows before him, his own voice broke with grief, and the tears even more than the applause of the whole audience bore witness alike to their feelings towards the exile, and the dramatic power of the actor. "He pleaded my cause before the Roman people", says Cicero (for it is he that tells the story), "with far more weight of eloquence than I could have pleaded for myself". [1]

[Footnote 1: Defence of Sestius, c. 56, &c.]

He had been visited with a remarkable dream, while staying with one of his friends in Italy, during the earlier days of his exile, which he now recalled with some interest. He tells us this story also himself, though he puts it into the mouth of another speaker, in his dialogue on "Divination". If few were so fond of introducing personal anecdotes into every place where he could find room for them, fewer still could tell them so well.

"I had lain awake a great part of the night, and at last towards dawn had begun to sleep soundly and heavily. I had given orders to my attendant that, in this case, though we had to start that very morning, strict silence should be kept, and that I was on no account to be disturbed; when about seven o'clock I awoke, and told him my dream. I thought I was wandering alone in some solitary place, when Caius Marius appeared to me, with his fasces bound with laurel, and asked why I was so sad? And when I answered that I had been driven from my country, he caught my hand, bade me be of good cheer, and put me under the guidance of his own lictor to lead me to his monument; there, he said, I should find my deliverance".

So indeed it had turned out. The temple dedicated to Honour and Virtue, in which the Senate sat when they passed the first resolution for Cicero's recall, was known as the "Monument of Marius". There is no need to doubt the perfect good faith of the story which he tells, and it may be set down as one of the earliest authenticated instances of a dream coming true. But if dreams are fashioned out of our waking imaginations, it is easy to believe that the fortunes of his great townsman Marius, and the scenes in the Senate at Rome, were continually present to the exile's thoughts.

His return was a triumphal progress. He landed at Brundusium on his daughter's birthday. She had only just lost her husband Piso, who had gallantly maintained her father's cause throughout, but she was the first to welcome him with tears of joy which overmastered her sorrow. He was careful to lose no chance of making his return impressive. He took his way to Rome with the slow march of a conqueror. The journey which Horace made easily in twelve days, occupied Cicero twenty-four. But he chose not the shortest but the most public route, through Naples, Capua, Minturnae, Terracina, and Aricia.

Let him tell the story of his own reception. If he tells it (as he does more than once) with an undisguised pride, it is a pride with which it is impossible not to sympathise. He boasted afterwards that he had been "carried back to Rome on the shoulders of Italy; " and Plutarch says it was a boast he had good right to make.

"Who does not know what my return home was like? How the people of Brundusium held out to me, as I might say, the right hand of welcome on behalf of all my native land? From thence to Rome my progress was like a march of all Italy. There was no district, no town, corporation, or colony, from which a public deputation was not sent to congratulate me. Why need I speak of my arrival at each place? how the people crowded the streets in the towns; how they flocked in from the country—fathers of families with wives and children? How can I describe those days, when all kept holiday, as though it were some high festival of the immortal gods, in joy for my safe return? That single day was to me like immortality; when I returned to my own city, when I saw the Senate and the population of all ranks come forth to greet me, when Rome herself looked as though she had wrenched herself from her foundations to rush to embrace her preserver. For she received me in such sort, that not only all sexes, ages, and callings, men and women, of every rank and degree, but even the very walls, the houses, the temples, seemed to share the universal joy".

The Senate in a body came out to receive him on the Appian road; a gilded chariot waited for him at the city gates; the lower class of citizens crowded the steps of the temples to see him as he passed;

and so he rode, escorted by troops of friends, more than a conqueror, to the Capitol.

His exultation was naturally as intense as his despair had been. He made two of his most florid speeches (if indeed they be his, which is doubtful), one in the Senate and another to the people assembled in the Forum, in which he congratulated himself on his return, and Rome on having regained her most illustrious citizen. It is a curious note of the temper and logical capacities of the mob, in all ages of the world alike, that within a few hours of their applauding to the echo this speech of Cicero's, Clodius succeeded in exciting them to a serious riot by appealing to the ruinous price of corn as one of the results of the exile's return.

For nearly four years more, though unable to shake Cicero's recovered position in the state—for he was now supported by Pompey—Clodius and his partisans, backed by a strong force of trained gladiators in their pay, kept Rome in a state of anarchy which is almost inexplicable. It was more than suspected that Crassus, now utterly estranged from Pompey, supplied out of his enormous wealth the means of keeping on foot this lawless agitation. Elections were overawed, meetings of the Senate interrupted, assassinations threatened and attempted. Already men began to look to military rule, and to think a good cause none the worse for being backed by "strong battalions". Things were fast tending to the point where Pompey and Caesar, trusty allies as yet in profession and appearance, deadly rivals at heart, hoped to step in with their veteran legions. Even Cicero, the man of peace and constitutional statesman, felt comfort in the thought that this final argument could be resorted to by his own party. But Clodius's mob-government, at any rate, was to be put an end to somewhat suddenly. Milo, now one of the candidates for the consulship, a man of determined and unscrupulous character, had turned his own weapons against him, and maintained an opposition patrol of hired gladiators and wild-beast fighters. The Senate quite approved, if they did not openly sanction, this irregular championship of their order. The two parties walked the streets of Rome like the Capulets and Montagues at Verona; and it was said that Milo had been heard to swear that he would rid the city of Clodius if he ever got the chance. It came at last, in a casual meeting on the Appian road, near Bovillae. A scuffle began between their retainers, and Clodius was killed—his friends said, murdered. The excitement at Rome was intense: the dead body was carried and laid publicly on the Rostra. Riots ensued; Milo was obliged to fly, and renounce his hopes of power; and the Senate, intimidated, named Pompey—not indeed "Dictator", for the name had become almost as hateful as that of King—but sole consul, for the safety of the state.

Cicero had resumed his practice as an advocate, and was now called upon to defend Milo. But Pompey, either from some private grudge, or in order to win favour with the populace, determined that Milo should be convicted. The jury were overawed by his presence in person at the trial, and by the occupation by armed soldiers of all the avenues of the court under colour of keeping order. It was really as great an outrage upon the free administration of justice as the presence of a regiment of soldiers at the entrance to Westminster Hall would be at a modern trial for high treason or sedition. Cicero affected to see in Pompey's legionaries nothing more than the maintainers of the peace of the city. But he knew better; and the fine passage in the opening of his speech for the defence, as it has come down to us, is at once a magnificent piece of irony, and a vindication of the rights of counsel.

"Although I am conscious, gentlemen, that it is a disgrace to me to show fear when I stand here to plead in behalf of one of the bravest of men; —and especially does such weakness ill become me, that when Milo himself is far more anxious about the safety of the state than about his own, I should be unable to bring to his defence the like magnanimous spirit; —yet this strange scene and strangely constituted court does terrify my eyes, for, turn them where I will, I look in vain for the ancient customs of the Forum, and the old style of public trials. For your tribunal to-day is girt with no such audience as was wont; this is no ordinary crowd that hems us in. Yon guards whom you see on duty in front of all the temples, though set to prevent violence, yet still do a sort of violence to the pleader; since in the Forum and the count of justice, though the military force which surrounds us be wholesome and needful, yet we cannot even be thus freed from apprehension without looking with some apprehension on the means. And if I thought they were set there in hostile array against Milo, I would yield to circumstances, gentlemen, and feel there was no room for the pleader amidst such a display of weapons. But I am encouraged by the advice of a man of great wisdom and justice—of Pompey, who surely would not think it compatible with that justice, after committing a prisoner to the verdict of a jury, then to hand him over to the swords of his soldiers; nor consonant with his wisdom to arm the violent passions of a mob with the authority of the state. Therefore those weapons, those officers and men, proclaim to us not peril but protection; they encourage us to be not only undisturbed but confident; they promise me not only support in pleading for the defence, but silence for it to be listened to. As to the rest of the audience, so far as it is composed of peaceful citizens, all, I know, are on our side; nor is there any single man among all those crowds whom you see occupying every point from which a glimpse of this court can be gained, looking on in anxious expectation of the result of this trial, who, while he approves the boldness of the defendant, does not also feel that the fate of himself, his children, and his country, hangs upon the issue of to-day".

After an elaborate argument to prove that the slaying of Clodius by Milo was in self-defence, or, at the worst, that it was a fate which he well deserved as a public enemy, he closes his speech with a peroration, the pathos of which has always been admired:

"I would it had been the will of heaven—if I may say so with all reverence for my country, for I fear lest my duty to my client may make me say what is disloyal towards her—I would that Publius Clodius were not only alive, but that he were praetor, consul, dictator even, before my eyes had seen this sight! But what says Milo? He speaks like a brave man, and a man whom it is your duty to protect—'Not so—by no means', says he. 'Clodius has met the doom he well deserved: I am ready, if it must be so, to meet that which I do not deserve'.... But I must stop; I can no longer speak for tears; and tears are an argument which he would scorn for his defence. I entreat you, I adjure you, ye who sit here in judgment, that in your verdict you dare to give utterance to what I know you feel".

But the appeal was in vain, or rather, as far as we can ascertain, was never made, —at least in such powerful terms as those in which we read it. The great advocate was wholly unmanned by the scene before him, grew nervous, and broke down utterly in his speech for the defence. This presence of a military force under the orders of Pompey—the man in whom he saw, as he hoped, the good genius of Rome—overawed and disturbed him. The speech which we read is almost certainly not that which he delivered, but, as in the previous case of Verres, the finished and elaborate composition of his calmer hours. Milo was convicted by a large majority; in fact, there can be little doubt but that he was legally guilty, however political expediency might, in the eyes of Cicero and his party, have justified his deed. Cato sat on the jury, and did all he could to insure an acquittal, showing openly his voting-paper to his fellow jurors, with that scorn of the "liberty of silence" which he shared with Cicero.

Milo escaped any worse penalty by at once going into voluntary banishment at Marseilles. But he showed more practical philosophy than his advocate; for when he read the speech in his exile, he is said to have declared that "it was fortunate for him it was not spoken, or he should never have known the flavour of the red mullet of Marseilles".

The removal of Clodius was a deliverance upon which Cicero never ceased to congratulate himself. That "battle of Bovillae", as he terms it, became an era in his mental records of only less significance than his consulship. His own public life continued to be honourable and successful. He was elected into the College of Augurs, an honour which he had long coveted; and he was appointed to the government of Cilicia. This latter was a greatness literally "thrust upon him", and which he would gladly have declined, for it took him away in these eventful days from his beloved Rome; and to these grand opportunities for enriching himself he was, as has been said, honourably indifferent. The appointment to a distant province was, in fact, to a man like Cicero, little better than an honourable form of exile: it was like conferring on a man who had been, and might hope one day to be again, Prime Minister of England, the governor-generalship of Bombay.

One consolation he found on reaching his new government—that even in the farthest wilds of Cilicia there were people who had heard of "the consul who saved Rome". And again the astonished provincials marvelled at a governor who looked upon them as having rights of their own, and neither robbed nor ill-used them. He made a little war, too, upon some troublesome hill-tribes (intrusting the command chiefly to his brother Quintus, who had served with distinction under Caesar in Gaul), and gained a victory which his legions thought of sufficient importance to salute him with the honoured title of "imperator". Such military honours are especially flattering to men who, like Cicero, are naturally and essentially civilians; and to Cicero's vanity they were doubly delightful. Unluckily they led him to entertain hopes of the further glory of a triumph; and this, but for the revolution which followed, he might possibly have obtained. As it was, the only result was his parading about with him everywhere, from town to town, for months after his return, the lictors with laurelled fasces, which betokened that a triumph was claimed—a pompous incumbrance, which became, as he confessed, a grand subject for evil-disposed jesters, and a considerable inconvenience to himself.

CHAPTER V.

CICERO AND CAESAR.

The future master of Rome was now coming home, after nearly ten years' absence, at the head of the victorious legions with which he had struck terror into the Germans, overrun all Spain, left his mark upon Britain, and "pacified" Gaul. But Cicero, in common with most of the senatorial party, failed to see in Julius Caesar the great man that he was. He hesitated a little—Caesar would gladly have had his support, and made him fair offers; but when the Rubicon was crossed, he threw in his lot with Pompey. He was certainly influenced in part by personal attachment: Pompey seems to have exercised a degree of fascination over his weakness. He knew Pompey's indecision of character, and confessed that Caesar was "a prodigy of energy; " but though the former showed little liking for him, he clung to him nevertheless. He foreboded that, let the contest end which way it would, "the result would certainly be a despotism". He foresaw that Pompey's real designs were as dangerous to the liberties of Rome as any of which Caesar could be suspected. "*Sullaturit animus*", he says of him in one of his letters, coining a verb to put his idea strongly—"he wants to be like Sulla". And it was no more than the truth. He found out afterwards, as he tells Atticus, that proscription-lists of all Caesar's adherents had been prepared by Pompey and his partisans, and that his old friend's name figured as one of the victims. Only this makes it possible to forgive him for the little feeling that he showed when he heard of Pompey's own miserable end.

Cicero's conduct and motives at this eventful crisis have been discussed over and over again. It may be questioned whether at this date we are in any position to pass more than a very cautious and general judgment upon them. We want all the "state papers" and political correspondence of the day—not Cicero's letters only, but those of Caesar and Pompey and Lentulus, and much information besides that was never trusted to pen or paper—in order to lay down with any accuracy the course which a really unselfish patriot could have taken. But there seems little reason to accuse Cicero of double-dealing or trimming in the worst sense. His policy was unquestionably, from first to last, a policy of expedients. But expediency is, and must be more or less, the watchword of a statesman. If he would practically serve his country, he must do to some extent what Cicero professed to do—make friends with those in power. *"Sic vivitur"*—"So goes the world; " *"Tempori serviendum est"*—"We must bend to circumstances"—these are not the noblest mottoes, but they are acted upon continually by the most respectable men in public and private life, who do not open their hearts to their friends so unreservedly as Cicero does to his friend Atticus. It seemed to him a choice between Pompey and Caesar; and he probably hoped to be able so far to influence the former, as to preserve some shadow of a constitution for Rome. What he saw in those "dregs of a Republic", [1] as he himself calls it, that was worth preserving; —how any honest despotism could seem to him more to be dreaded than that prostituted liberty, —this is harder to comprehend. The remark of Abeken seems to go very near the truth—"His devotion to the commonwealth was grounded not so much upon his conviction of its actual merits, as of its fitness for the display of his own abilities".

[Footnote 1: "Faex Romuli".]

But that commonwealth was past saving even in name. Within two months of his having been declared a public enemy, all Italy was at Caesar's feet. Before another year was past, the battle of Pharsalia had been fought, and the great Pompey lay a headless corpse on the sea-shore in Egypt. It was suggested to Cicero, who had hitherto remained constant to the fortunes of his party, and was then in their camp at Dyrrachium, that he should take the chief command, but he had the sense to decline; and though men called him "traitor", and drew their swords upon him, he withdrew from a cause which he saw was lost, and returned to Italy, though not to Rome.

The meeting between him and Caesar, which came at last, set at rest any personal apprehensions from that quarter. Cicero does not appear to have made any dishonourable submission, and the conqueror's behaviour was nobly forgetful of the past. They gradually became on almost friendly terms. The orator paid the Dictator compliments in the Senate, and found that, in private society, his favourite jokes were repeated to the great man, and were highly appreciated. With such little successes he was obliged now to be content. He had again taken up his residence in Rome; but his political occupation was gone, and his active mind had leisure to employ itself in some of his literary works.

It was at this time that the blow fell upon him which prostrated him for the time, as his exile had done, and under which he claims our far more natural sympathy. His dear daughter Tullia—again married, but unhappily, and just divorced—died at his Tusculan villa. Their loving intercourse had undergone no change from her childhood, and his grief was for a while inconsolable. He shut himself up for thirty days. The letters of condolence from well-meaning friends were to him—as they so often are—as the speeches of the three comforters to Job. He turned in vain, as he pathetically says, to philosophy for consolation.

It was at this time that he wrote two of his philosophical treatises, known to us as 'The True Ends of Life', [1] and the 'Tusculan Disputations', of which more will be said hereafter. In this latter, which he named from his favourite country-house, he addressed himself to the subjects which suited best with his own sorrowful mood under his recent bereavement. How men might learn to shake off the terrors of death—nay, to look upon it rather as a release from pain and evil; how pain, mental and bodily, may best be borne; how we may moderate our passions; and, lastly, whether the practice of virtue be not all-sufficient for our happiness.

[Footnote 1: 'De Finibus Bonorum et Malorum'—a title hard to translate.]

A philosopher does not always find in himself a ready pupil. It was hardly so in Cicero's case. His arguments were incontrovertible; but he found them fail him sadly in their practical application to life. He never could shake off from himself that dread of death which he felt in a degree unusually vivid for a Roman. He sought his own happiness afterwards, as he had done before, rather in the exciting struggle of public life than in the special cultivation of any form of virtue; and he did not even find the remedy for his present domestic sorrow in any of those general moral reflections which philosophy, Christian as well as pagan, is so ready to produce upon such occasions; which are all so undeniable, and all so utterly unendurable to the mourner.

Cicero found his consolation, or that diversion of thought which so mercifully serves the purpose of consolation, where most men of active minds like his seek for it and find it—in hard work. The literary effort of writing and completing the works which have been just mentioned probably did more to soothe his mind than all the arguments which they contained. He resumed his practice as an advocate so far as to plead a cause before Caesar, now ruling as Dictator at Rome—the last cause, as events happened, that he was ever to plead. It was a cause of no great importance—a defence of Deiotarus, titulary king of Armenia, who was accused of having entertained designs against the life of Caesar while entertaining him as a guest in his palace. The Dictator reserved his judgment until he should have made his campaign against the Parthians. That more convenient season never came: for before the spring campaign could open, the fatal "Ides of March" cut short Caesar's triumphs and his life.

CHAPTER VI.

CICERO AND ANTONY.

It remained for Cicero yet to take a part in one more great national struggle — the last for Rome and for himself. No doubt there was some grandeur in the cause which he once more so vigorously espoused — the recovery of the liberties of Rome. But all the thunders of Cicero's eloquence, and all the admiration of modern historians and poets, fail to enlist our hearty sympathies with the assassins of Caesar. That "consecration of the dagger" to the cause of liberty has been the fruitful parent of too much evil ever since to make its use anything but hateful. That Cicero was among the actual conspirators is probably not true, though his enemies strongly asserted it. But at least he gloried in the deed when done, and was eager to claim all the honours of a tyrannicide. Nay, he went farther than the actual conspirators, in words at least; it is curious to find him so careful to disclaim complicity in the act. "Would that you had invited me to that banquet on the Ides of March! there would then have been no leavings from the feast", — he writes to Cassius. He would have had their daggers turned on Antony, at all events, as well as on Caesar. He wishes that "the gods may damn Caesar after he is dead; " professing on this occasion a belief in a future retribution, on which at other times he was sceptical. It is but right to remember all this, when the popular tide turned, and he himself came to be denounced to political vengeance. The levity with which he continually speaks of the assassination of Caesar — a man who had never treated *him*, at any rate, with anything but a noble forbearance — is a blot on Cicero's character which his warmest apologists admit.

The bloody deed in the Capitol was done — a deed which was to turn out almost what Goethe called it — "the most absurd that ever was committed". The great Dictator who lay there alone, a "bleeding piece of earth", deserted by the very men who had sought of late to crown him, was perhaps Rome's fittest master; certainly not the worst of the many with whom a personal ambition took the place of principle. Three slaves took up the dead body of their master, and carried it home to his house. Poor wretches! they knew nothing about liberty or the constitution; they had little to hope, and probably little to fear; they had only a humble duty to do, and did it. But when we read of them, and of that freedman who, not long before, sat by the dead body of Pompey till he could scrape together wreck from the shore to light some sort of poor funeral-pile, we return with a shudder of disgust to those "noble Romans" who occupy at this time the foreground of history.

Caesar had been removed, but it is plain that Brutus and Cassius and their party had neither the ability nor the energy to make any real use of their bloody triumph. Cicero soon lost all hope of seeing in them the liberators of his country, or of being able to guide himself the revolution which he hoped he had seen begun. "We have been freed", he writes to Atticus, "but we are not free". "We have struck down the tyrant, but the tyranny survives". Antony, in fact, had taken the place of Caesar as master of Rome—a change in all respects for the worse. He had surrounded himself with guards; had obtained authority from the Senate to carry out all decrees and orders left by the late Dictator; and when he could not find, amongst Caesar's memoranda, materials to serve his purpose, he did not hesitate to forge them. Cicero had no power, and might be in personal danger, for Antony knew his sentiments as to state matters generally, and more particularly towards himself. Rome was no longer any place for him, and he soon left it—this time a voluntary exile. He wandered from place to place, and tried as before to find interest and consolation in philosophy. It was now that he wrote his charming essays on 'Friendship' and on 'Old Age', and completed his work 'On the Nature of the Gods', and that on 'Divination'. His treatise 'De Officiis' (a kind of pagan 'Whole Duty of Man') is also of this date, as well as some smaller philosophical works which have been lost. He professed himself hopeless of his country's future, and disgusted with political life, and spoke of going to end his days at Athens.

But, as before and always, his heart was in the Forum at Rome. Political life was really the only atmosphere in which he felt himself breathe vigorously. Unquestionably he had also an earnest patriotism, which would have drawn him back to his country's side at any time when he believed that she had need of his help. He was told that he was needed there now; that there was a prospect of matters going better for the cause of liberty; that Antony was coming to terms of some kind with the party of Brutus, —and he returned.

For a short while these latter days brought with them a gleam of triumph almost as bright as that which had marked the overthrow of Catiline's conspiracy. Again, on his arrival at Rome, crowds rushed to meet him with compliments and congratulations, as they had done some thirteen years before. And in so far as his last days were spent in resisting to the utmost the basest of all Rome's bad men, they were to him greater than any triumph. Thenceforth it was a fight to the death between him and Antony; so long as Antony lived, there could be no liberty for Rome. Cicero left it to his enemy to make the first attack. It soon came. Two days after his return, Antony spoke vehemently in the Senate against him, on the occasion of moving a resolution to the effect that divine honours should be paid to Caesar. Cicero had purposely stayed away, pleading fatigue after his journey; really, because such a proposition was odious to him. Antony denounced him as a coward and a traitor, and threatened to send men to pull down his house about his head — that house which had once before been pulled down, and rebuilt for him by his remorseful fellow-citizens. Cicero went down to the Senate the following day, and there delivered a well-prepared speech, the first of those fourteen which are known to us as his 'Philippics' — a name which he seems first to have given to them in jest, in remembrance of those which his favourite model Demosthenes had delivered at Athens against Philip of Macedon. He defended his own conduct, reviewed in strong but moderate terms the whole policy of Antony, and warned him — still ostensibly as a friend — against the fate of Caesar. The speaker was not unconscious what his own might possibly be.

"I have already, senators, reaped fruit enough from my return home, in that I have had the opportunity to speak words which, whatever may betide, will remain in evidence of my constancy in my duty, and you have listened to me with much kindness and attention. And this privilege I will use so often as I may without peril to you and to myself; when I cannot, I will be careful of myself, not so much for my own sake as for the sake of my country. For me, the life that I have lived seems already well-nigh long enough, whether I look at my years or my honours; what little span may yet be added to it should be your gain and the state's far more than my own".

Antony was not in the house when Cicero spoke; he had gone down to his villa at Tibur. There he remained for a fortnight, brooding over his reply — taking lessons, it was said, from professors in the art of rhetorical self-defence. At last he came to Rome and answered his opponent. His speech has not reached us; but we know that it contained the old charges of having put Roman citizens to death without trial in the case of the abettors of Catiline, and of having instigated Milo to the assassination of Clodias. Antony added a new charge—that of complicity with the murderers of Caesar. Above all, he laughed at Cicero's old attempts as a poet; a mode of attack which, if not so alarming, was at least as irritating as the rest. Cicero was not present—he dreaded personal violence; for Antony, like Pompey at the trial of Milo, had planted an armed guard of his own men outside and inside the Senate-house. Before Cicero had nerved himself to reply, Antony had left Rome to put himself at the head of his legions, and the two never met again.

The reply, when it came, was the terrible second Philippic; never spoken, however, but only handed about in manuscript to admiring friends. There is little doubt, as Mr. Long observes, that Antony had also some friend kind enough to send him a copy; and if we may trust the Roman poet Juvenal, who is at least as likely to have been well informed upon the subject as any modern historian, this composition eventually cost the orator his life. It is not difficult to understand the bitter vindictiveness of Antony. Cicero had been not merely a political opponent; he had attacked his private character (which presented abundant grounds for such attack) with all the venom of his eloquence. He had said, indeed, in the first of these powerful orations, that he had never taken this line.

"If I have abused his private life and character, I have no right to complain if he is my enemy: but if I have only followed my usual custom, which I have ever maintained in public life, —I mean, if I have only spoken my opinion on public questions freely, —then, in the first place, I protest against his being angry with me at all: or, if this be too much to expect, I demand that he should be angry with me only as with a fellow-citizen".

If there had been any sort of reticence on this point hitherto on the part of Cicero, he made up for it in this second speech. Nothing can equal its bitter personality, except perhaps its rhetorical power. He begins the attack by declaring that he will not tell all he knows—"in order that, if we have to do battle again hereafter, I may come always fresh-armed to the attack; an advantage which the multiplicity of that man's crimes and vices gives me in large measure". Then he proceeds:

"Would you like us, then, to examine into your course of life from boyhood? I conclude you would. Do you remember that before you put on the robe of manhood, you were a bankrupt? That was my father's fault, you will say. I grant it—it is a defence that speaks volumes for your feelings as a son. It was your own shamelessness, however, that made you take your seat in the stalls of honourable knights, whereas by law there is a fixed place for bankrupts, even when they have become so by fortune's fault, and not their own. You put on the robe which was to mark your manhood, —on your person it became the flaunting gear of a harlot".

It is not desirable to follow the orator through some of his accusations; when he had to lash a man whom he held to be a criminal, he did not much care where or how he struck. He even breaks off himself—after saying a good deal.

"There are some things, which even a decent enemy hesitates to speak of.... Mark, then, his subsequent course of life, which I will trace as rapidly as I can. For though these things are better known to you than even to me, yet I ask you to hear me with attention—as indeed you do; for it is right that in such cases men's feelings should be roused not merely by the knowledge of the facts, but by calling them back to their remembrance; though we must dash at once, I believe, into the middle of his history, lest we should be too long in getting to the end".

The peroration is noble and dignified, in the orator's best style. He still supposes himself addressing his enemy. He has warned Antony that Caesar's fate may be his: and he is not unconscious of the peril in which his own life may stand.

"But do you look to yourself—I will tell you how it stands with me. I defended the Commonwealth when I was young—I will not desert it now I am old. I despised the swords of Catiline—I am not likely to tremble before yours. Nay, I shall lay my life down gladly, if the liberty of Rome can be secured by my death, so that this suffering nation may at last bring to the birth that which it his long been breeding. [1] If, twenty years ago, I declared in this house that death could never be said to have come before its time to a man who had been consul of Rome, with how much more truth, at my age, may I say it now! To me indeed, gentlemen of the Senate, death may well be a thing to be even desired, when I have done what I have done and reaped the honours I have reaped. Only two wishes I have, — the one, that at my death I may leave the Roman people free—the immortal gods can give me no greater boon than this; the other, that every citizen may meet with such reward as his conduct towards the state may have deserved".

[Footnote 1: *I. e.*, the making away with Antony.]

The publication of this unspoken speech raised for the time an enthusiasm against Antony, whom Cicero now openly declared to be an enemy to the state. He hurled against him Philippic after Philippic. The appeal at the end of that which comes the sixth in order is eloquent enough.

"The time is come at last, fellow-citizens; somewhat too late, indeed, for the dignity of the people of Rome, but at least the crisis is so ripe, that it cannot now be deferred an instant longer. We have had one calamity sent upon us, as I may say, by fate, which we bore with—in such sort as it might be borne. If another befalls us now, it will be one of our own choosing. That this Roman people should serve any master, when the gods above have willed us to be the masters of the world, is a crime in the sight of heaven. The question hangs now on its last issue. The struggle is for our liberties. You must either conquer, Romans, —and this, assuredly, with such patriotism and such unanimity as I see here, you must do, or you must endure anything and everything rather than be slaves. Other nations may endure the yoke of slavery, but the birthright of the people of Rome is liberty".

Antony had left Rome, and thrown himself, like Catiline, into the arms of his soldiers, in his province of Cisalpine Gaul. There he maintained himself in defiance of the Senate, who at last, urged by Cicero, declared him a public enemy. Caesar Octavianus (great-nephew of Julius) offered his services to the state, and with some hesitation they were accepted. The last struggle was begun. Intelligence soon arrived that Antony had been defeated at Mutina by the two last consuls of the Republic, Hirtius and Pansa. The news was dashed, indeed, afterwards by the further announcement that both consuls had died of their wounds. But it was in the height of the first exultation that Cicero addressed to the Senate his fourteenth Philippic—the last oration which he was ever to make. For the moment, he found himself once more the foremost man at Rome. Crowds of roaring patriots had surrounded his house that morning, escorted him in triumph up to the Capitol, and back to his own house, as they had done in the days of his early glory. Young Caesar, who had paid him much personal deference, was professing himself a patriot; the Commonwealth was safe again—and Cicero almost thought that he again himself had saved it.

But Rome now belonged to those who had the legions. It had come to that: and when Antony succeeded in joining interests with Octavianus (afterwards miscalled Augustus)—"the boy", as both Cicero and Antony called him—a boy in years as yet, but premature in craft and falsehood—who had come "to claim his inheritance", and succeeded in rousing in the old veterans of his uncle the desire to take vengeance a on his murderers, the fate of the Republic and of Cicero was sealed.

It was on a little eyot formed by the river Reno, near Bologna, that Antony, young Caesar, and Lepidus (the nominal third in what is known as the Second Triumvirate) met to arrange among themselves the division of power, and what they held to be necessary, to the securing it for the future—the proscription of their several enemies. No private affections or interests were to be allowed to interfere with this merciless arrangement. If Lepidus would give up his brother, Antony would surrender an obnoxious uncle. Octavianus made a cheaper sacrifice in Cicero, whom Antony, we may be sure, with those terrible Philippics ringing in his ears, demanded with an eager vengeance. All was soon amicably settled; the proscription-lists were made out, and the Triumvirate occupied Rome.

Cicero and his brother—whose name was known to be also on the fatal roll—heard of it while they were together at the Tusculan villa. Both took immediate measures to escape. But Quintus had to return to Rome to get money for their flight, and, as it would appear, to fetch his son. The emissaries of the Triumvirate were sent to search the house: the father had hid himself, but the son was seized, and refusing to give any information, was put to the torture. His father heard his cries of agony, came forth from his hiding-place, and asked only to be put to death first. The son in his turn made the same request, and the assassins were so far merciful that they killed both at once.

Cicero himself might yet have escaped, but for some thing of his old indecision. He had gone on board a small vessel with the intention of joining Brutus in Macedonia, when he suddenly changed his mind, and insisted on being put on shore again. He wandered about, half-resolving (for the third) time on suicide. He would go to Rome, stab himself on the altar-hearth in young Caesar's house, and call down the vengeance of heaven upon the traitor. The accounts of these last hours of his life are, unfortunately, somewhat contradictory, and none of the authorities to be entirely depended on; Abeken has made a careful attempt to harmonise them, which it will be best here to follow.

Urged by the prayers of his slaves, the faithful adherents of a kind master, he once more embarked, and once more (Appian says, from sea-sickness, which he never could endure) landed near Caieta, where be had a seaside villa. Either there, or, as other accounts say, at his house at Formiae, he laid himself down to pass the night, and wait for death. "Let me die", said he, "in my own country, which I have so often saved". But again the faithful slaves aroused him, forced him into a litter, and hurried him down through the woods to the sea-shore—for the assassins were in hot pursuit of him. They found his house shut up; but some traitor showed them a short cut by which to overtake the fugitive. As he lay reading (it is said), even during these anxious moments, a play of his favourite Euripides, every line of whom he used to declare contained some maxim worth remembering, he heard their steps approaching, and ordered the litter to be set down. He looked out, and recognised at the head of the party an officer named Laenas, whom he had once successfully defended on a capital charge; but he saw no gratitude or mercy in the face, though there were others of the band who covered their eyes for pity, when they saw the dishevelled grey hair and pale worn features of the great Roman (he was within a month of sixty-four). He turned from Laenas to the centurion, one Herennius, and said, "Strike, old soldier, if you understand your trade! " At the third blow—by one or other of those officers, for both claimed the evil honour—his head was severed. They carried it straight to Antony, where he sat on the seat of justice in the Forum, and demanded the offered reward. The triumvir, in his joy, paid it some ten times over. He sent the bloody trophy to his wife; and the Roman Jezebel spat in the dead face, and ran her bodkin through the tongue which had spoken those bold and bitter truths against her false husband. The great orator fulfilled, almost in the very letter, the words which, treating of the liberty of the pleader, he had put into the mouth of Crassus—"You must cut out this tongue, if you would check my free speech: nay, even then, my very breathing should protest against your lust for power". The head, by Antony's order, was then nailed upon the Rostra, to speak there, more eloquently than ever the living lips had spoken, of the dead liberty of Rome.

CHAPTER VII.

CHARACTER AS A POLITICIAN AND AN ORATOR.

Cicero shared very largely in the feeling which is common to all men of ambition and energy, —a desire to stand well not only with their own generation, but with posterity. It is a feeling natural to every man who knows that his name and acts must necessarily become historical. If it is more than usually patent in Cicero's case, it is only because in his letters to Atticus we have more than usual access to the inmost heart of the writer; for surely such a thoroughly confidential correspondence has never been published before or since. "What will history say of me six hundred years hence? " he asks, unbosoming himself in this sort to his friend. More than thrice the six hundred years have passed, and, in Cicero's case, history has hardly yet made up its mind. He has been lauded and abused, from his own times down to the present, in terms as extravagant as are to be found in the most passionate of his own orations; both his accusers and his champions have caught the trick of his rhetorical exaggeration more easily than his eloquence. Modern German critics like Drumann and Mommsen have attacked him with hardly less bitterness, though with more decency, than the historian Dio Cassius, who lived so near his own times. Bishop Middleton, on the other hand, in those pleasant and comprehensive volumes which are still to this day the great storehouse of materials for Cicero's biography, is as blind to his faults as though he were himself delivering a panegyric in the Rostra at Rome. Perhaps it is the partiality of the learned bishop's view which has produced a reaction in the minds of sceptical German scholars, and of some modern writers of our own. It is impossible not to sympathise in some degree with that Athenian who was tired of always hearing Aristides extolled as "the Just; " and there was certainly a strong temptation to critics to pick holes in a man's character who was perpetually, during his lifetime and for eighteen centuries after his death, having a trumpet sounded before him to announce him as the prince of patriots as well as philosophers; worthy indeed, as Erasmus thought, to be canonised as a saint of the Catholic Church, but for the single drawback of his not having been a Christian.

On one point some of his eulogists seem manifestly unfair. They say that the circumstances under which we form our judgment of the man are exceptional in this—that we happen to possess in his case all this mass of private and confidential letters (there are nearly eight hundred of his own which have come down to us), giving us an insight into his private motives, his secret jealousies, and hopes, and fears, and ambitions, of which in the case of other men we have no such revelation. It is quite true; but his advocates forget that it is from the very same pages which reveal his weaknesses, that they draw their real knowledge of many of those characteristics which they most admire—his sincere love for his country, his kindness of heart, his amiability in all his domestic relations. It is true that we cannot look into the private letters of Caesar, or Pompey, or Brutus, as we can into Cicero's; but it is not so certain that if we could, our estimate of their characters would be lowered. We might discover, in their cases as in his, many traces of what seems insincerity, timidity, a desire to sail with the stream; we might find that the views which they expressed in public were not always those which they entertained in private; but we might also find an inner current of kindness, and benevolence, and tenderness of heart, for which the world gives them little credit. One enthusiastic advocate, Wieland, goes so far as to wish that this kind of evidence could, in the case of such a man as Cicero, have been "cooked", to use a modern phrase: that we could have had only a judicious selection from this too truthful mass, of correspondence; that his secretary, Tiro, or some judicious friend, had destroyed the whole packet of letters in which the great Roman bemoaned himself, during his exile from Rome, to his wife, to his brother, and to Atticus. The partisan method of writing history, though often practised, has seldom been so boldly professed.

But it cannot be denied, that if we know too much of Cicero to judge him merely by his public life, as we are obliged to do with so many heroes of history, we also know far too little of those stormy times in which he lived, to pronounce too strongly upon his behaviour in such difficult circumstances. The true relations between the various parties at Rome, as we have tried to sketch them, are confessedly puzzling even to the careful student. And without a thorough understanding of these, it is impossible to decide, with any hope of fairness, upon Cicero's conduct as a patriot and a politician. His character was full of conflicting elements, like the times in which he lived, and was necessarily in a great degree moulded by them. The egotism which shows itself so plainly alike in his public speeches and in his private writings, more than once made him personal enemies, and brought him into trouble, though it was combined with great kindness of heart and consideration for others. He saw the right clearly, and desired to follow it, but his good intentions were too often frustrated by a want of firmness and decision. His desire to keep well with men of all parties, so long as it seemed possible (and this not so much from the desire of self-aggrandisement, as from a hope through their aid to serve the commonwealth) laid him open on more than one occasion to the charge of insincerity.

There is one comprehensive quality which may be said to lave been wanting in his nature, which clouded his many excellences, led him continually into false positions, and even in his delightful letters excites in the reader, from time to time, an impatient feeling of contempt. He wanted manliness. It was a quality which was fast dying out, in his day, among even the best of the luxurious and corrupt aristocracy of Rome. It was perhaps but little missed in his character by those of his contemporaries who knew and loved him best. But without that quality, to an English mind, it is hard to recognise in any man, however brilliant and amiable, the true philosopher or hero.

The views which this great Roman politician held upon the vexed question of the ballot did not differ materially from those of his worthy grandfather before-mentioned. [1] The ballot was popular at Rome, —for many reasons, some of them not the most creditable to the characters of the voters; and because it was popular, Cicero speaks of it occasionally, in his forensic speeches, with a cautious praise; but of his real estimate of it there can be no kind of doubt. "I am of the same opinion now", he writes to his brother, "that ever I was; there is nothing like the open suffrage of the lips". So in one of his speeches, he uses even stronger language: "The ballot", he says, "enables men to open their faces, and to cover up their thoughts; it gives them licence to promise whatever they are asked, and at the same time to do whatever they please". Mr. Grote once quoted a phrase of Cicero's, applied to the voting-papers of his day, as a testimony in favour of this mode of secret suffrage—grand words, and wholly untranslatable into anything like corresponding English—"*Tabella vindex tacitae libertatis*"—"the tablet which secures the liberty of silence". But knowing so well as Cicero did what was the ordinary character of Roman jurors and Roman voters, and how often this "liberty of silence" was a liberty to take a bribe and to vote the other way, one can almost fancy that we see upon his lips, as he utters the sounding phrase, that playful curve of irony which is said to have been their characteristic expression. [2] Mr. Grote forgot, too, as was well pointed out by a writer in the 'Quarterly Review', [3] that in the very next sentence the orator is proud to boast that he himself was not so elected to office, but "by the living voices" of his fellow-citizens.

[Footnote 1: See p. 3.]

[Footnote 2: No bust, coin, or gem is known which bears any genuine likeness of Cicero. There are several existing which purport to be such, but all are more or less apocryphal.]

[Footnote 3: Quart. Rev., lxi. 522.]

The character of his eloquence may be understood in some degree by the few extracts which have been given from his public speeches; always remembering how many of its charms are necessarily lost by losing the actual language in which his thoughts were clothed. We have lost perhaps nearly as much in another way, in that we can only read the great orator instead of listening to him. Yet it is possible, after all, that this loss to us is not so great as it might seem. Some of his best speeches, as we know—those, for instance, against Verres and in defence of Milo—were written in the closet, and never spoken at all; and most of the others were reshaped and polished for publication. Nor is it certain that his declamation, which some of his Roman rivals found fault with as savouring too much of the florid Oriental type, would have been agreeable to our colder English taste. He looked upon gesture and action as essential elements of the orator's power, and had studied them carefully from the artists of the theatre. There can be no doubt that we have his own views on this point in the words which he has put into the mouth of his "Brutus", in the treatise on oratory which bears that name. He protests against the "Attic coldness" of style which, he says, would soon empty the benches of their occupants. He would have the action and bearing of the speaker to be such that even the distant spectator, too far off to hear, should "know that there was a Roscius on the stage". He would have found a French audience in this respect more sympathetic than an English one. [1] His own highly nervous temperament would certainly tend to excited action. The speaker, who, as we are told, "shuddered visibly over his whole body when he first began to speak", was almost sure, as he warmed to his work, to throw himself into it with a passionate energy.

[Footnote 1: Our speakers certainly fall into the other extreme. The British orator's style of gesticulation may still be recognised, *mutatis mutandis*, in Addison's humorous sketch of a century ago: "You may see many a smart rhetorician turning his hat in his hands, moulding it into several different cocks, examining sometimes the lining and sometimes the button, during the whole course of his harangue. A deaf man would think that he was cheapening a beaver, when he is talking perhaps of the fate of the British nation".]

He has put on record his own ideas of the qualifications and the duties of the public speaker, whether in the Senate or at the bar, in three continuous treatises on the subject, entitled respectively, 'On Oratory', 'Brutus', and 'The Orator', as well as in some other works of which we have only fragments remaining. With the first of these works, which he inscribed to his brother, he was himself exceedingly well satisfied, and it perhaps remains still the ablest, as it was the first, attempt to reduce eloquence to a science. The second is a critical sketch of the great orators of Rome: and in the third we have Cicero's view of what the perfect orator should be. His ideal is a high one, and a true one; that he should not be the mere rhetorician, any more than the mere technical lawyer or keen partisan, but the man of perfect education and perfect taste, who can speak on all subjects, out of the fulness of his mind, "with variety and copiousness".

Although, as has been already said, he appears to have attached but little value to a knowledge of the technicalities of law, in other respects his preparation for his work was of the most careful kind; if we may assume, as we probably may, that it is his own experience which, in his treatise on Oratory, he puts into the mouth of Marcus Antonius, one of his greatest predecessors at the Roman bar.

"It is my habit to have every client explain to me personally his own case; to allow no one else to be present, that so he may speak more freely. Then I take the opponent's side, while I make him plead his own cause, and bring forward whatever arguments he can think of. Then, when he is gone, I take upon myself, with as much impartiality as I can, three different characters—my own, my opponent's, and that of the jury. Whatever point seems likely to help the case rather than injure it, this I decide must be brought forward; when I see that anything is likely to do more harm than good, I reject and throw it aside altogether. So I gain this, —that I think over first what I mean to say, and speak afterwards; while a good many pleaders, relying on their abilities, try to do both at once". [1]

[Footnote 1: De Oratore, II. 24, 72.]

He reads a useful lesson to young and zealous advocates in the same treatise—that sometimes it may be wise not to touch at all in reply upon a point which makes against your client, and to which you have no real answer; and that it is even more important to say nothing which may injure your case, than to omit something which might possibly serve it. A maxim which some modern barristers (and some preachers also) might do well to bear in mind.

Yet he did not scorn to use what may almost be called the tricks of his art, if he thought they would help to secure him a verdict. The outward and visible appeal to the feelings seems to have been as effective in the Roman forum as with a British jury. Cicero would have his client stand by his side dressed in mourning, with hair dishevelled, and in tears, when he meant to make a pathetic appeal to the compassion of the jurors; or a family group would be arranged, as circumstances allowed, —the wife and children, the mother and sisters, or the aged father, if presentable, would be introduced in open court to create a sensation at the right moment. He had tears apparently as ready at his command as an eloquent and well-known English Attorney-General. Nay, the tears seem to have been marked down, as it were, upon his brief. "My feelings prevent my saying more", he declares in his defence of Publius Sylla. "I weep while I make the appeal"—"I cannot go on for tears"—he repeats towards the close of that fine oration in behalf of Milo—the speech that never was spoken. Such phrases remind us of the story told of a French preacher, whose manuscripts were found to have marginal stage directions: "Here take out your handkerchief; "—"here cry—if possible". But such were held to be the legitimate adjuncts of Roman oratory, and it is quite possible to conceive that the advocate, like more than one modern tragedian who could be named, entered so thoroughly into the spirit of the part that the tears flowed quite naturally.

A far less legitimate weapon of oratory—offensive and not defensive—was the bitter and coarse personality in which he so frequently indulged. Its use was held perfectly lawful in the Roman forum, whether in political debate or in judicial pleadings, and it was sure to be highly relished by a mixed audience. There is no reason to suppose that Cicero had recourse to it in any unusual degree; but employ it he did, and most unscrupulously. It was not only private character that he attacked, as in the case of Antony and Clodius, but even personal defects or peculiarities were made the subject of bitter ridicule. He did not hesitate to season his harangue by a sarcasm on the cast in the prosecutor's eye, or the wen on the defendant's neck, and to direct the attention of the court to these points, as though they were corroborative evidence of a moral deformity. The most conspicuous instance of this practice of his is in the invective which he launched in the Senate against Piso, who had made a speech reflecting upon him. Referring to Cicero's exile, he had made that sore subject doubly sore by declaring that it was not Cicero's unpopularity, so much as his unfortunate propensity to bad verse, which had been the cause of it. A jingling line of his to the effect that

"The gown wins grander triumphs than the sword"[1]

had been thought to be pointed against the recent victories of Pompey, and to have provoked him to use his influence to get rid of the author. But this annotation of Cicero's poetry had not been Piso's only offence. He had been consul at the time of the exile, and had given vent, it may be remembered, to the witticism that the "saviour of Rome" might save the city a second time by his absence. Cicero was not the man to forget it. The beginning of his attack on Piso is lost, but there is quite enough remaining. Piso was of a swarthy complexion, approaching probably to the negro type. "Beast" — is the term by which Cicero addresses him. "Beast! there is no mistaking the evidence of that slave-like hue, those bristly cheeks, those discoloured fangs. Your eyes, your brows, your face, your whole aspect, are the tacit index to your soul". [2]

[Footnote 1: "Cedant arma togae, concedat laurea linguae".]

[Footnote 2: Such flowers of eloquence are not encouraged at the modern bar. But they were common enough, even in the English law-courts, in former times. Mr. Attorney-General Coke's language to Raleigh at his trial—"Thou viper! "—comes quite up to Cicero's. Perhaps the Irish House of Parliament, while it existed, furnished the choicest modern specimens of this style of oratory. Mr. O'Flanagan, in his 'Lives of the Lord Chancellors of Ireland', tells us that a member for Galway, attacking an opponent when he knew that his sister was present during the debate, denounced the whole family— "from the toothless old hag that is now grinning in the gallery, to the white-livered scoundrel that is shivering on the floor".]

It is not possible, within the compass of these pages, to give even the briefest account of more than a few of the many causes (they are twenty-four in number) in which the speeches made by Cicero, either for the prosecution or the defence, have been preserved to us. Some of them have more attraction for the English reader than others, either from the facts of the case being more interesting or more easily understood, or from their affording more opportunity for the display of the speaker's powers.

Mr. Fox had an intense admiration for the speech in defence of Caelius. The opinion of one who was no mean orator himself, on his great Roman predecessor, may be worth quoting:

"Argumentative contention is not what he excels in; and he is never, I think, so happy as when he has an opportunity of exhibiting a mixture of philosophy and pleasantry, and especially when he can interpose anecdotes and references to the authority of the eminent characters in the history of his own country. No man appears, indeed, to have had such a real respect for authority as he; and therefore when he speaks on that subject he is always natural and earnest". [1]

[Footnote 1: Letter to G. Wakefield—Correspondence, p. 35.]

There is anecdote and pleasantry enough in this particular oration; but the scandals of Roman society of that day, into which the defence of Caelius was obliged to enter, are not the most edifying subject for any readers. Caelius was a young man of "equestrian" rank, who had been a kind of ward of Cicero's, and must have given him a good deal of trouble by his profligate habits, if the guardianship was anything more than nominal. But in this particular case the accusation brought against him—of trying to murder an ambassador from Egypt by means of hired assassins, and then to poison the lady who had lent him the money to bribe them with—was probably untrue. Clodia, the lady in question, was the worthy sister of the notorious Clodius, and bore as evil a reputation as it was possible for a woman to bear in the corrupt society of Rome—which is saying a great deal. She is the real mover in the case, though another enemy of Caelius, the son of a man whom he had himself brought to trial for bribery, was the ostensible prosecutor. Cicero, therefore, throughout the whole of his speech, aims the bitter shafts of his wit and eloquence at Clodia. His brilliant invectives against this lady, who was, as he pointedly said, "not only noble but notorious", are not desirable to quote. But the opening of the speech is in the advocate's best style. The trial, it seems, took place on a public holiday, when it was not usual to take any cause unless it were of pressing importance.

"If any spectator be here present, gentlemen, who knows nothing of our laws, our courts of justice, or our national customs, he will not fail to wonder what can be the atrocious nature of this case, that on a day of national festival and public holiday like this, when all other business in the Forum is suspended, this single trial should be going on; and he will entertain no doubt but that the accused is charged with a crime of such enormity, that if it were not at once taken cognisance of, the constitution itself would be in peril. And if he heard that there was a law which enjoined that in the case of seditious and disloyal citizens who should take up arms to attack the Senate-house, or use violence against the magistrates, or levy war against the commonwealth, inquisition into the matter should be made at once, on the very day; —he would not find fault with such a law: he would only ask the nature of the charge. But when he heard that it was no such atrocious crime, no treasonable attempt, no violent outrage, which formed the subject of this trial, but that a young man of brilliant abilities, hard-working in public life, and of popular character, was here accused by the son of a man whom he had himself once prosecuted, and was still prosecuting, and that all a bad woman's wealth and influence was being used against him, —he might take no exception to the filial zeal of Atratinus; but he would surely say that woman's infamous revenge should be baffled and punished.... I can excuse Atratinus; as to the other parties, they deserve neither excuse nor forbearance".

It was a strange story, the case for the prosecution, especially as regarded the alleged attempt to poison Clodia. The poison was given to a friend of Caelius, he was to give it to some slaves of Clodia whom he was to meet at certain baths frequented by her, and they were in some way to administer it. But the slaves betrayed the secret; and the lady employed certain gay and profligate young men, who were hangers-on of her own, to conceal themselves somewhere in the baths, and pounce upon Caelius's emissary with the poison in his possession. But this scheme was said to have failed. Clodia's detectives had rushed from their place of concealment too soon, and the bearer of the poison escaped. The counsel for the prisoner makes a great point of this.

"Why, 'tis the catastrophe of a stage-play—nay, of a burlesque; when no more artistic solution of the plot can be invented, the hero escapes, the bell rings, and—the curtain falls! For I ask why, when Licinius was there trembling, hesitating, retreating, trying to escape—why that lady's body-guard let him go out of their hands? Were they afraid lest, so many against one, such stout champions against a single helpless man, frightened as he was and fierce as they were, they could not master him? I should like exceedingly to see them, those curled and scented youths, the bosom-friends of this rich and noble lady; those stout men-at-arms who were posted by their she-captain in this ambuscade in the baths. And I should like to ask them how they hid themselves, and where? A bath? —why, it must rather have been a Trojan horse, which bore within its womb this band of invincible heroes who went to war for a woman! I would make them answer this question, —why they, being so many and so brave, did not either seize this slight stripling, whom you see before you, where he stood, or overtake him when he fled? They will hardly be able to explain themselves, I fancy, if they get into that witness-box, however clever and witty they may be at the banquet, —nay, even eloquent occasionally, no doubt, over their wine. But the air of a court of justice is somewhat different from that of the banquet-hall; the benches of this court are not like the couches of a supper-table; the array of this jury presents a different spectacle from a company of revellers; nay, the broad glare of sunshine is harder to face than the glitter of the lamps. If they venture into it, I shall have to strip them of their pretty conceits and fools' gear. But, if they will be ruled by me, they will betake themselves to another trade, win favour in another quarter, flaunt themselves elsewhere than in this court. Let them carry their brave looks to their lady there; let them lord it at her expense, cling to her, lie at her feet, be her slaves; only let them make no attempt upon the life and honour of an innocent man".

The satellites of Clodia could scarcely have felt comfortable under this withering fire of sarcasm. The speaker concluded with an apology—much required—for his client's faults, as those of a young man, and a promise on his behalf—on the faith of an advocate—that he would behave better for the future. He wound up the whole with a point of sensational rhetoric which was common, as has been said, to the Roman bar as to our own—an appeal to the jurymen as fathers. He pointed to the aged father of the defendant, leaning in the most approved attitude upon the shoulder of his son. Either this, or the want of evidence, or the eloquence of the pleader, had its due effect. Caelius was triumphantly acquitted; and it is a proof that the young man was not wholly graceless, that he rose afterwards to high public office, and never forgot his obligations to his eloquent counsel, to whom he continued a stanch friend. He must have had good abilities, for he was honoured with frequent letters from Cicero when the latter was governor of Cilicia. He kept up some of his extravagant tastes; for when he was Aedile (which involved the taking upon him the expense of certain gladiatorial and wild-beast exhibitions), he wrote to beg his friend to send him out of his province some panthers for his show. Cicero complied with the request, and took the opportunity, so characteristic of him, of lauding his own administration of Cilicia, and making a kind of pun at the same time. "I have given orders to the hunters to see about the panthers; but panthers are very scarce, and the few there are complain, people say, that in the whole province there are no traps laid for anybody but for them". Catching and skinning the unfortunate provincials, which had been a favourite sport with governors like Verres, had been quite done away with in Cilicia, we are to understand, under Cicero's rule.

His defence of Ligarius, who was impeached of treason against the state in the person of Caesar, as having borne arms against him in his African campaign, has also been deservedly admired. There was some courage in Cicero's undertaking his defence; as a known partisan of Pompey, he was treading on dangerous and delicate ground. Caesar was dictator at the time; and the case seems to have been tried before him as the sole judicial authority, without pretence of the intervention of anything like a jury. The defence—if defence it may be called—is a remarkable instance of the common appeal, not to the merits of the case, but to the feelings of the court. After making out what case he could for his client, the advocate as it were throws up his brief, and rests upon the clemency of the judge. Caesar himself, it must be remembered, had begun public life, like Cicero, as a pleader: and, in the opinion of some competent judges, such as Tacitus and Quintilian, had bid fair to be a close rival.

"I have pleaded many causes, Caesar—some, indeed, in association with yourself, while your public career spared you to the courts; but surely I never yet used language of this sort, —'Pardon him, sirs, he has offended: he has made a false step: he did not think to do it; he never will again'. This is language we use to a father. To the court it must be, —'He did not do it: he never contemplated it: the evidence is false; the charge is fabricated'. If you tell me you sit but as the judge of the fact in this case, Caesar, —if you ask me where and when he served against you, —I am silent; I will not now dwell on the extenuating circumstances, which even before a judicial tribunal might have their weight. We take this course before a judge, but I am here pleading to a father. 'I have erred—I have done wrong, I am sorry: I take refuge in your clemency; I ask forgiveness for my fault; I pray you, pardon me'.... There is nothing so popular, believe me, sir, as kindness; of all your many virtues none wins men's admiration and their love like mercy. In nothing do men reach so near the gods, as when they can give life and safety to mankind. Fortune has given you nothing more glorious than the power, your own nature can supply nothing more noble than the will, to spare and pardon wherever you can. The case perhaps demands a longer advocacy— your gracious disposition feels it too long already. So I make an end, preferring for my cause that you should argue with your own heart, than that I or any other should argue with you. I will urge nothing more than this, —the grace which you shall extend to my client in his absence, will be felt as a boon by all here present".

The great conqueror was, it is said, visibly affected by the appeal, and Ligarius was pardoned.

CHAPTER VIII.

MINOR CHARACTERISTICS.

Not content with his triumphs in prose, Cicero had always an ambition—to be a poet. Of his attempts in this way we have only some imperfect fragments, scattered here and there through his other works, too scanty to form any judgment upon. His poetical ability is apt to be unfairly measured by two lines which his opponents were very fond of quoting and laughing at, and which for that reason have become the best known. But it is obvious that if Wordsworth or Tennyson were to be judged solely by a line or two picked out by an unfavourable reviewer—say from 'Peter Bell' or from the early version of the 'Miller's Daughter'—posterity would have a very mistaken appreciation of their merits. Plutarch and the younger Pliny, who had seen more of Cicero's poetry than we have, thought highly of it. So he did himself; but so it was his nature to think of most of his own performances; and such an estimate is common to other authors besides Cicero, though few announce it so openly. Montaigne takes him to task for this, with more wit, perhaps, than fairness. "It is no great fault to write poor verses; but it is a fault not to be able to see how unworthy such poor verses were of his reputation". Voltaire, on the other hand, who was perhaps as good a judge, thought there was "nothing more beautiful" than some of the fragments of his poem on 'Marius', who was the ideal hero of his youth. Perhaps the very fact, however, of none of his poems having been preserved, is some argument that such poetic gift as he had was rather facility than genius. He wrote, besides this poem on 'Marius', a 'History of my Consulship', and a 'History of my Own Times', in verse, and some translations from Homer.

He had no notion of what other men called relaxation: he found his own relaxation in a change of work. He excuses himself in one of his orations for this strange taste, as it would seem to the indolent and luxurious Roman nobles with whom he was so unequally yoked.

"Who after all shall blame me, or who has any right to be angry with me, if the time which is not grudged to others for managing their private business, for attending public games and festivals, for pleasures of any other kind, —nay, even for very rest of mind and body, —the time which others give to convivial meetings, to the gaming-table, to the tennis-court, —this much I take for myself, for the resumption of my favourite studies? "

In this indefatigable appetite for work of all kinds, he reminds us of no modern politician so much as of Sir George Cornewall Lewis; yet he would not have altogether agreed with him in thinking that life would be very tolerable if it were not for its amusements. He was, as we have seen, of a naturally social disposition. "I like a dinner-party", he says in a letter to one of his friends; "where I can say just what comes uppermost, and turn my sighs and sorrows into a hearty laugh. I doubt whether you are much better yourself, when you can laugh as you did even at a philosopher. When the man asked— 'Whether anybody wanted to know anything? ' you said you had been wanting to know all day when it would be dinner-time. The fellow expected you to say you wanted to know how many worlds there were, or something of that kind". [1]

[Footnote 1: These professional philosophers, at literary dinner-parties, offered to discuss and answer any question propounded by the company.]

He is said to have been a great laugher. Indeed, he confesses honestly that the sense of humour was very powerful with him—"I am wonderfully taken by anything comic", he writes to one of his friends. He reckons humour also as a useful ally to the orator. "A happy jest or facetious turn is not only pleasant, but also highly useful occasionally; " but he adds that this is an accomplishment which must come naturally, and cannot be taught under any possible system. [1] There is at least sufficient evidence that he was much given to making jokes, and some of them which have come down to us would imply that a Roman audience was not very critical on this point. There is an air of gravity about all courts of justice which probably makes a very faint amount of jocularity hailed as a relief. Even in an English law-court, a joke from the bar, much more from the bench, does not need to be of any remarkable brilliancy in order to be secure of raising a laugh; and we may fairly suppose that the same was the case at Rome. Cicero's jokes were frequently nothing more than puns, which it would be impossible, even if it were worth while, to reproduce to an English ear. Perhaps the best, or at all events the most intelligible, is his retort to Hortensius during the trial of Verres. The latter was said to have feed his counsel out of his Sicilian spoils—especially, there was a figure of a sphinx, of some artistic value, which had found its way from the house of the ex-governor into that of Hortensius. Cicero was putting a witness through a cross-examination of which his opponent could not see the bearing. "I do not understand all this", said Hortensius; "I am no hand at solving riddles". "That is strange, too", rejoined Cicero, "when you have a sphinx at home". In the same trial he condescended, in the midst of that burning eloquence of which we have spoken, to make two puns on the defendant's name. The word "*Verres*" had two meanings in the old Latin tongue: it signified a "boar-pig", and also a "broom" or "sweeping-brush". One of Verres's friends, who either was or had the reputation of being a Jew, had tried to get the management of the prosecution out of Cicero's hands. "What has a Jew to do with *pork*? " asked the orator. Speaking, in the course of the same trial, of the way in which the governor had made "requisitions" of all the most valuable works of art throughout the island, "the broom", said he, "swept clean". He did not disdain the comic element in poetry more than in prose; for we find in Quinitilian [2] a quotation from a punning epigram in some collection of such trifles which in his time bore Cicero's name. Tiro is said to have collected and published three volumes of his master's good things after his death; but if they were not better than those which have come down to us, as contained in his other writings, there has been no great loss to literature in Tiro's 'Ciceroniana'. He knew one secret at least of a successful humourist in society: for it is to him that we owe the first authoritative enunciation of a rule which is universally admitted—"that a jest never has so good an effect as when it is uttered with a serious countenance".

[Footnote 1: De Orat. II. 54.]

[Footnote 2: 'Libellus Jocularis', Quint. viii. 6.]

Cicero had a wonderful admiration for the Greeks. "I am not ashamed to confess", he writes to his brother, "especially since my life and career have been such that no suspicion of indolence or want of energy can rest upon me, that all my own attainments are due to those studies and those accomplishments which have been handed down to us in the literary treasures and the philosophical systems of the Greeks". It was no mere rhetorical outburst, when in his defence of Valerius Flaccus, accused like Verres, whether truly or falsely, of corrupt administration in his province, he thus introduced the deputation from Athens and Lacedaemon who appeared as witnesses to the character of his client.

"Athenians are here to-day, amongst whom civilisation, learning, religion, agriculture, public law and justice, had their birth, and whence they have been disseminated over all the world: for the possession of whose city, on account of its exceeding beauty, even gods are said to have contended: which is of such antiquity, that she is said to have bred her citizens within herself, and the same soil is termed at once their mother, their nurse, and their country: whose importance and influence is such that the name of Greece, though it has lost much of its weight and power, still holds its place by virtue of the renown of this single city".

He had forgotten, perhaps, as an orator is allowed to forget, that in the very same speech, when his object was to discredit the accusers of his client, he had said, what was very commonly said of the Greeks at Rome, that they were a nation of liars. There were excellent men among them, he allowed—thinking at the moment of the counter-evidence which he had ready for the defendant—but he goes on to make this sweeping declaration:

"I will say this of the whole race of the Greeks: I grant them literary genius, I grant them skill in various accomplishments, I do not deny them elegance in conversation, acuteness of intellect, fluent oratory; to any other high qualities they may claim I make no objection: but the sacred obligation that lies upon a witness to speak the truth is what that nation has never regarded". [1]

[Footnote 1: Defence of Val. Flaccus, c. 4.]

There was a certain proverb, he went on to say, "Lend me your evidence", implying—"and you shall have mine when you want it; " a Greek proverb, of course, and men knew these three words of Greek who knew no Greek besides. What he loved in the Greeks, then, was rather the grandeur of their literature and the charm of their social qualities (a strict regard for truth is, unhappily, no indispensable ingredient in this last); he had no respect whatever for their national character. The orator was influenced, perhaps, most of all by his intense reverence for the Athenian Demosthenes, whom, as a master in his art, he imitated and well-nigh worshipped. The appreciation of his own powers which every able man has, and of which Cicero had at least his share, fades into humility when he comes to speak of his great model. "Absolutely perfect", he calls him in one place; and again in another, "What I have attempted, Demosthenes has achieved". Yet he felt also at times, when the fervour of genius was strong within him, that there was an ideal of eloquence enshrined in his own inmost mind, "which I can *feel*", he says, "but which I never knew to exist in any man".

He could not only write Greek as a scholar, but seems to have spoken it with considerable ease and fluency; for on one occasion he made a speech in that language, a condescension which some of his friends thought derogatory to the dignity of a Roman.

From the Greeks he learnt to appreciate art. How far his taste was really cultivated in this respect is difficult for us to judge. Some passages in his letters to Atticus might lead us to suspect that, as Disraeli concludes, he was rather a collector than a real lover of art. His appeals to his friend to buy up for him everything and anything, and his surrender of himself entirely to Atticus's judgment in such purchases, do not bespeak a highly critical taste. In a letter to another friend, he seems to say that he only bought statuary as "furniture" for the gymnasium at his country-seat; and he complains that four figures of Bacchanals, which this friend had just bought for him, had cost more than he would care to give for all the statues that ever were made. On the other hand, when he comes to deal with Verres's wholesale plunder of paintings and statues in Sicily, he talks about the several works with considerable enthusiasm. Either he really understood his subject, or, like an able advocate, he had thoroughly got up his brief. But the art-notices which are scattered through his works show a considerable acquaintance with the artist-world of his day. He tells us, in his own admirable style, the story of Zeuxis, and the selection which he made from all the beauties of Crotona, in order to combine their several points of perfection in his portrait of Helen; he refers more than once, and always in language which implies an appreciation of the artist, to the works of Phidias, especially that which is said to have cost him his life—the shield of Minerva; and he discusses, though it is but by way of illustration, the comparative points of merit in the statues of Calamis, and Myron, and Polycletus, and in the paintings of the earlier schools of Zeuxis, Polygnotus, and Timanthes, with their four primitive colours, as compared with the more finished schools of Protogenes and Apelles.

CHAPTER IX.

CICERO'S CORRESPONDENCE.

I. ATTICUS.

It seems wonderful how, in the midst of all his work, Cicero found time to keep up such a voluminous correspondence. Something like eight hundred of his letters still remain to us, and there were whole volumes of them long preserved which are now lost, [1] to say nothing of the very many which may never have been thought worth preserving. The secret lay in his wonderful energy and activity. We find him writing letters before day-break, during the service of his meals, on his journeys, and dictating them to an amanuensis as he walked up and down to take needful exercise.

[Footnote 1: Collections of his letters to Caesar, Brutus, Cornelius Nepos the historian, Hirtius, Pansa, and to his son, are known to have existed.]

His correspondents were of almost all varieties of position and character, from Caesar and Pompey, the great men of the day, down to his domestic servant and secretary, Tiro. Amongst them were rich and ease-loving Epicureans like Atticus and Paetus, and even men of pleasure like Caelius: grave Stoics like Cato, eager patriots like Brutus and Cassius, authors such as Cornelius Nepos and Lucceius the historians, Varro the grammarian, and Metius the poet; men who dabbled with literature in a gentleman-like way, like Hirtius and Appius, and the accomplished literary critic and patron of the day— himself of no mean reputation as poet, orator, and historian—Caius Asinius Pollio. Cicero's versatile powers found no difficulty in suiting the contents of his own letters to the various tastes and interests of his friends. Sometimes he sends to his correspondent what was in fact a political journal of the day—rather one-sided, it must be confessed, as all political journals are, but furnishing us with items of intelligence which throw light, as nothing else can, on the history of those latter days of the Republic. Sometimes he jots down the mere gossip of his last dinner-party; sometimes he notices the speculations of the last new theorist in philosophy, or discusses with a literary friend some philological question—the latter being a study in which he was very fond of dabbling, though with little success, for the science of language was as yet unknown.

His chief correspondent, as has been said, was his old school-fellow and constant friend through life, Pomponius Atticus. The letters addressed to him which still remain to us cover a period of twenty-four years, with a few occasional interruptions, and the correspondence only ceased with Cicero's death. The Athenianised Roman, though he had deliberately withdrawn himself from the distracting factions of his native city, which he seldom revisited, kept on the best terms with the leaders of all parties, and seems to have taken a very lively interest, though merely in the character of a looker-on, in the political events which crowded so fast upon each other during the fifty years of his voluntary expatriation. Cicero's letters were to him what an English newspaper would be now to an English gentleman who for his own reasons preferred to reside in Paris, without forswearing his national interests and sympathies. At times, when Cicero was more at leisure, and when messengers were handy (for we have to remember that there was nothing like our modern post), Cicero would despatch one of these letters to Atticus daily. We have nearly four hundred of them in all. They are continually garnished, even to the point of affectation, with Greek quotations and phrases, partly perhaps in compliment to his friend's Athenian tastes, and partly from the writer's own passion for the language.

So much reference has been made to them throughout the previous biographical sketch, —for they supply us with some of the most important materials for Cicero's life and times, —that it may be sufficient to give in this place two or three of the shorter as specimens of the collection. One which describes a visit which he received from Julius Caesar, already dictator, in his country-house near Puteoli, is interesting, as affording a glimpse behind the scenes in those momentous days when no one knew exactly whether the great captain was to turn out a patriot or a conspirator against the liberties of Rome.

"To think that I should have had such a tremendous visitor! But never mind; for all went off very pleasantly. But when he arrived at Philippus's house[1] on the evening of the second day of the Saturnalia, the place was so full of soldiers that they could hardly find a spare table for Caesar himself to dine at. There were two thousand men. Really I was in a state of perplexity as to what was to be done next day: but Barba Cassius came to my aid, —he supplied me with a guard. They pitched their tents in the grounds, and the house was protected. He stayed with Philippus until one o'clock on the third day of the Saturnalia, and would see no one. Going over accounts, I suppose, with Balbus. Then he walked on the sea-shore. After two he had a bath: then he listened to some verses on Mamurra, without moving a muscle of his countenance: then dressed, [2] and sat down to dinner. He had taken a precautionary emetic, and therefore ate and drank heartily and unrestrainedly. We had, I assure you, a very good dinner, and well served; and not only that, but

'The feast of reason and the flow of soul'[3]

besides. His suite were abundantly supplied at three other tables: the freedmen of lower rank, and even the slaves, were well taken care of. The higher class had really an elegant entertainment. Well, no need to make a long story; we found we were both 'flesh and blood'. Still he is not the kind of guest to whom you would say—'Now do, pray, take us in your way on your return'. Once is enough. We had no conversation on business, but a good deal of literary talk. In short, he seemed to be much pleased, and to enjoy himself. He said he should stay one day at Puteoli, and another at Baiae. So here you have an account of this visit, or rather quartering of troops upon me, which I disliked the thoughts of, but which really, as I have said, gave me no annoyance. I shall stay here a little longer, then go to my house at Tusculum. When Caesar passed Dolabella's villa, all the troops formed up on the right and left of his horse, which they did nowhere else. [4] I heard that from Nicias".

[Footnote 1: This was close to Cicero's villa, on the coast.]

[Footnote 2: Literally, "he got himself oiled". The emetic was a disgusting practice of Roman *bon vivants* who were afraid of indigestion.]

[Footnote 3: The verse which Cicero quotes from Lucilius is fairly equivalent to this.]

[Footnote 4: Probably by way of salute; or possibly as a precaution.]

In the following, he is anticipating a visit from his friend, and from the lady to whom he is betrothed.

"I had a delightful visit from Cincius on the 30th of January, before daylight. For he told me that you were in Italy, and that he was going to send off some messengers to you, and would not let them go without a letter from me. Not that I have much to write about (especially when you are all but here), except to assure you that I am anticipating your arrival with the greatest delight. Therefore fly to me, to show your own affection, and to see what affection I bear you. Other matters when we meet. I have written this in a hurry. As soon as ever you arrive, bring all your people to my house. You will gratify me very much by coming. You will see how wonderfully well Tyrannio has arranged my books, the remains of which are much better than I had thought. And I should be very glad if you could send me a couple of your library clerks whom Tyrannio could make use of as binders, and to help him in other ways; and tell them to bring some parchment to make indices—syllabuses, I believe you Greeks call them. But this only if quite convenient to you. But, at any rate, be sure you come yourself, if you can make any stay in our parts, and bring Pilia with you, for that is but fair, and Tullia wishes it much. Upon my word you have bought a very fine place. I hear that your gladiators fight capitally. If you had cared to hire them out, you might have cleared your expenses at these two last public shows. But we can talk about this hereafter. Be sure to come; and do your best about the clerks, if you love me".

The Roman gentleman of elegant and accomplished tastes, keeping a troop of private gladiators, and thinking of hiring them out, to our notions, is a curious combination of character; but the taste was not essentially more brutal than the prize-ring and the cock-fights of the last century.

II. PAETUS.

Another of Cicero's favourite correspondents was Papirius Paetus, who seems to have lived at home at ease, and taken little part in the political tumults of his day. Like Atticus, he was an Epicurean, and thought more of the pleasures of life than of its cares and duties. Yet Cicero evidently took great pleasure in his society, and his letters to him are written in the same familiar and genial tone as those to his old school-fellow. Some of them throw a pleasant light upon the social habits of the day. Cicero had had some friends staying with him at his country-seat at Tusculum, to whom, he says, he had been giving lessons in oratory. Dolabella, his son-in-law, and Hirtius, the future consul, were among them. "They are my scholars in declamation, and I am theirs in dinner-eating; for I conclude you have heard (you seem to hear everything) that they come to me to declaim, and I go to them for dinners. 'Tis all very well for you to swear that you cannot entertain me in such grand fashion as I am used to, but it is of use…. Better be victimised by your friend than by your debtors, as you have been. After all, I don't require such a banquet as leaves a great waste behind it; a little will do, only handsomely served and well cooked. I remember your telling me about a dinner of Phamea's—well, it need not be such a late affair as that, nor so grand in other respects; nay, if you persist in giving me one of your mother's old family dinners, I can stand even that. My new reputation for good living has reached you, I find, before my arrival, and you are alarmed at it; but, pray, put no trust in your ante-courses—I have given up that altogether. I used to spoil my appetite, I remember, upon your oil and sliced sausages…. One expense I really shall put you to; I must have my warm bath. My other habits, I assure you, are quite unaltered; all the rest is joke".

Paetus seems to answer him with the same good-humoured badinage. Balbus, the governor of Africa, had been to see him, he says, and *he* had been content with such humble fare as he feared Cicero might despise. So much, at least, we may gather from Cicero's answer.

"Satirical as ever, I see. You say Balbus was content with very modest fare. You seem to insinuate that when grandees are so moderate, much more ought a poor ex-consul like myself so to be. You don't know that I fished it all out of your visitor himself, for he came straight to my house on his landing. The very first words I said to him were, 'How did you get on with our friend Paetus? ' He swore he had never been better entertained. If this referred to the charms of your conversation, remember, I shall be quite as appreciative a listener as Balbus; but if it meant the good things on the table, I must beg you will not treat us men of eloquence worse than you do a 'Lisper'". [1]

[Footnote 1: One of Cicero's puns. Balbus means 'Lisper'.]

They carry on this banter through several letters. Cicero regrets that he has been unable as yet to pay his threatened visit, when his friend would have seen what advances he had made in gastronomic science. He was able now to eat through the whole bill of fare— "from the eggs to the *roti*".

"I [Stoic that used to be] have gone over with my whole forces into the camp of Epicurus. You will have to do with a man who can eat, and who knows what's what. You know how conceited we late learners are, as the proverb says. You will have to unlearn those little 'plain dinners' and makeshifts of yours. We have made such advances in the art, that we have been venturing to invite, more than once, your friends Verrius and Camillus (what elegant and fastidious gentlemen they are!). But see how audacious we are getting! I have even given Hirtius a dinner—but without a peacock. My cook could imitate nothing in his entertainments except the hot soup".

Then he hears that his friend is in bed with the gout.

"I am extremely sorry to hear it, as in duty bound; still, I am quite determined to come, that I may see you, and pay my visit, —yes, and have my dinner: for I suppose your cook has not got the gout as well".

Such were the playful epistles of a busy man. But even in some of these lightest effusions we see the cares of the statesman showing through. Here is a portion of a later letter to the same friend.

"I am very much concerned to hear you have given up going out to dinner; for it is depriving yourself of a great source of enjoyment and gratification. Then, again, I am afraid—for it is as well to speak honestly—lest you should unlearn certain old habits of yours, and forget to give your own little dinners. For if formerly, when you had good examples to imitate, you were still not much of a proficient in that way, how can I suppose you will get on now? Spurina, indeed, when I mentioned the thing to him, and explained your previous habits, proved to demonstration that there would be danger to the highest interests of the state if you did not return to your old ways in the spring. But indeed, my good Paetus, I advise you, joking apart, to associate with good fellows, and pleasant fellows, and men who are fond of you. There is nothing better worth having in life, nothing that makes life more happy.... See how I employ philosophy to reconcile you to dinner-parties. Take care of your health; and that you will best do by going out to dinner.... But don't imagine, as you love me, that because I write jestingly I have thrown off all anxiety about public affairs. Be assured, my dear Paetus, that I seek nothing and care for nothing, night or day, but how my country may be kept safe and free. I omit no opportunity of advising, planning, or acting. I feel in my heart that if in securing this I have to lay down my life, I shall have ended it well and honourably".

III. HIS BROTHER QUINTUS.

Between Marcus Cicero and his younger brother Quintus there existed a very sincere and cordial affection—somewhat warmer, perhaps, on the side of the elder, inasmuch as his wealth and position enabled him rather to confer than to receive kindnesses; the rule in such cases being (so cynical philosophers tell us) that the affection is lessened rather than increased by the feeling of obligation. He almost adopted the younger Quintus, his nephew, and had him educated with his own son; and the two cousins received their earlier training together in one or other of Marcus Cicero's country-houses under a clever Greek freedman of his, who was an excellent scholar, and—what was less usual amongst his countrymen, unless Cicero's estimate of them does them great injustice—a very honest man, but, as the two boys complained, terribly passionate. Cicero himself, however, was the head tutor—an office for which, as he modestly writes, his Greek studies fully qualified him. Quintus Cicero behaved ill to his brother after the battle of Pharsalia, making what seem to have been very unjust accusations against him in order to pay court to Caesar; but they soon became friends again.

Twenty-nine of the elder Cicero's letters to his brother remain, written in terms of remarkable kindness and affection, which go far to vindicate the Roman character from a charge which has sometimes been brought against it of coldness in these family relationships. Few modern brothers, probably, would write to each other in such terms as these:

"Afraid lest your letters bother me? I wish you would bother me, and re-bother me, and talk to me and at me; for what can give me more pleasure? I swear that no muse-stricken rhymester ever reads his own last poem with more delight than I do what you write to me about matters public or private, town or country. Here now is a letter from you full of pleasant matter, but with this dash of the disagreeable in it, that you have been afraid—nay, are even now afraid—of being troublesome to me. I could quarrel with you about it, if that were not a sin. But if I have reason to suspect anything of that sort again, I can only say that I shall always be afraid lest, when we are together, I may be troublesome to you".

Or take, again, the pathetic apology which he makes for having avoided an interview with Quintus in those first days of his exile when he was so thoroughly unmanned:

"My brother, my brother, my brother! Did you really fear that I was angry, because I sent off the slaves without any letter to you? And did you even think that I was unwilling to see you? I angry with you? Could I possibly be angry with you?... When I miss you, it is not a brother only that I miss. To me you have always been the pleasantest of companions, a son in dutiful affection, a father in counsel. What pleasure ever had I without you, or you without me?"

Quintus had accompanied Caesar on his expedition into Britain as one of his lieutenants, and seems to have written home to his brother some notices of the country; to which the latter, towards the end of his reply, makes this allusion:

"How delighted I was to get your letter from Britain! I had been afraid of the voyage across, afraid of the rock-bound coast of the island. The other dangers of such a campaign I do not mean to despise, but in these there is more to hope than to fear, and I have been rather anxiously expecting the result than in any real alarm about it. I see you have a capital subject to write about. What novel scenery, what natural curiosities and remarkable places, what strange tribes and strange customs, what a campaign, and what a commander you have to describe! I will willingly help you in the points you request, and I will send you the verses you ask for— though it is sending 'an owl to Athens', [1] I know".

[Footnote 1: A Greek proverb, equivalent to our 'coals to Newcastle'.]

In another letter he says, "Only give me Britain to paint with your colours and my own pencil". But either the Britons of those days did not, after all, seem to afford sufficient interest for poem or history, or for some other reason this joint literary undertaking, which seems once to have been contemplated, was never carried out, and we have missed what would beyond doubt have been a highly interesting volume of Sketches in Britain by the brothers Cicero.

Quintus was a poet, as well as his brother—nay, a better poet, in the latter's estimation, or at least he was polite enough to say so more than once. In quantity, at least, if not in quality, the younger must have been a formidable rival, for he wrote, as appears from one of these letters, four tragedies in fifteen days—possibly translations only from the Greek.

One of the most remarkable of all Cicero's letters, and perhaps that which does him most credit both as a man and a statesman, is one which he wrote to his brother, who was at the time governor of Asia. Indeed, it is much more than a letter; it is rather a grave and carefully weighed paper of instructions on the duties of such a position. It is full of sound practical sense, and lofty principles of statesmanship—very different from the principles which too commonly ruled the conduct of Roman governors abroad. The province which had fallen to the lot of Quintus Cicero was one of the richest belonging to the Empire, and which presented the greatest temptations and the greatest facilities for the abuse of power to selfish purposes. Though called Asia, it consisted only of the late kingdom of Pergamus, and had come under the dominion of Rome, not by conquest, as was the case with most of the provinces, but by way of legacy from Attalus, the last of its kings; who, after murdering most of his own relations, had named the Roman people as his heirs. The seat of government was at Ephesus. The population was of a very mixed character, consisting partly of true Asiatics, and partly of Asiatic Greeks, the descendants of the old colonists, and containing also a large Roman element—merchants who were there for purposes of trade, many of them bankers and money-lenders, and speculators who farmed the imperial taxes, and were by no means scrupulous in the matter of fleecing the provincials. These latter—the 'Publicani', as they were termed—might prove very dangerous enemies to any too zealous reformer. If the Roman governor there really wished to do his duty, what with the combined servility and double-dealing of the Orientals, the proverbial lying of the Greeks, and the grasping injustice of the Roman officials, he had a very difficult part to play. How Quintus had been playing it is not quite clear. His brother, in this admirable letter, assumes that he had done all that was right, and urges him to maintain the same course. But the advice would hardly have been needed if all had gone well hitherto.

"You will find little trouble in holding your subordinates in check, if you can but keep a check upon yourself. So long as you resist gain, and pleasure, and all other temptations, as I am sure you do, I cannot fancy there will be any danger of your not being able to check a dishonest merchant or an extortionate collector. For even the Greeks, when they see you living thus, will look upon you as some hero from their old annals, or some supernatural being from heaven, come down into their province.

"I write thus, not to urge you so to act, but that you may congratulate yourself upon having so acted, now and heretofore. For it is a glorious thing for a man to have held a government for three years in Asia, in such sort that neither statue, nor painting, nor work of art of any kind, nor any temptations of wealth or beauty (in all which temptations your province abounds) could draw you from the strictest integrity and self-control: that your official progresses should have been no cause of dread to the inhabitants, that none should be impoverished by your requisitions, none terrified at the news of your approach; —but that you should have brought with you, wherever you came, the most hearty rejoicings, public and private, inasmuch as every town saw in you a protector and not a tyrant—every family received you as a guest, not as a plunderer.

"But in these points, as experience has by this time taught you, it is not enough for you to have these virtues yourself, but you must look to it carefully, that in this guardianship of the province not you alone, but every officer under you, discharges his duty to our subjects, to our fellow-citizens, and to the state.... If any of your subordinates seem grasping for his own interest, you may venture to bear with him so long as he merely neglects the rules by which he ought to be personally bound; never so far as to allow him to abuse for his own gain the power with which you have intrusted him to maintain the dignity of his office. For I do not think it well, especially since the customs of official life incline so much of late to laxity and corrupt influence, that you should scrutinise too closely every abuse, or criticise too strictly every one of your officers, but rather place trust in each in proportion as you feel confidence in his integrity.

"For those whom the state has assigned you as companions and assistants in public business, you are answerable only within the limits I have just laid down; but for those whom you have chosen to associate with yourself as members of your private establishment and personal suite, you will be held responsible not only for all they do, but for all they say....

"Your ears should be supposed to hear only what you publicly listen to, not to be open to every secret and false whisper for the sake of private gain. Your official seal should be not as a mere common tool, but as though it were yourself; not the instrument of other men's wills, but the evidence of your own. Your officers should be the agents of your clemency, not of their own caprice; and the rods and axes which they bear should be the emblems of your dignity, not merely of your power. In short, the whole province should feel that the persons, the families, the reputation, and the fortunes of all over whom you rule, are held by you very precious. Let it be well understood that you will hold that man as much your enemy who gives a bribe, if it comes to your knowledge, as the man who receives it. But no one will offer bribes, if this be once made clear, that those who pretend to have influence of this kind with you have no power, after all, to gain any favour for others at your hands.

* * * * *

"Let such, then, be the foundations of your dignity; —first, integrity and self-control on your own part; a becoming behaviour on the part of all about you; a very careful and circumspect selection of your intimates, whether Greeks or provincials; a grave and firm discipline maintained throughout your household. For if such conduct befits us in our private and everyday relations, it becomes well-nigh godlike in a government of such extent, in a state of morals so depraved, and in a province which presents so many temptations. Such a line of conduct and such rules will alone enable you to uphold that severity in your decisions and decrees which you have employed in some cases, and by which we have incurred (and I cannot regret it) the jealousy of certain interested parties.... You may safely use the utmost strictness in the administration of justice, so long as it is not capricious or partial, but maintained at the same level for all. Yet it will be of little use that your own decisions be just and carefully weighed, unless the same course be pursued by all to whom you delegate any portion of your judicial authority. Such firmness and dignity must be employed as may not only be above partiality, but above the suspicion of it. To this must be added readiness to give audience, calmness in deciding, care in weighing the merits of the case and in satisfying the claims of the parties".

Yet he advises that justice should be tempered with leniency.

"If such moderation be popular at Rome, where there is so much self-assertion, such unbridled freedom, so much licence allowed to all men; —where there are so many courts of appeal open, so many means of help, where the people have so much power and the Senate so much authority; how grateful beyond measure will moderation be in the governor of Asia, a province where all that vast number of our fellow-citizens and subjects, all those numerous states and cities, hang upon one man's nod! where there is no appeal to the tribune, no remedy at law, no Senate, no popular assembly. Wherefore it should be the aim of a great man, and one noble by nature and trained by education and liberal studies, so to behave himself in the exercise of that absolute power, as that they over whom he presides should never have cause to wish for any authority other than his".

IV. TIRO.

Of all Cicero's correspondence, his letters to Tiro supply the most convincing evidence of his natural kindness of heart. Tiro was a slave; but this must be taken with some explanation. The slaves in a household like Cicero's would vary in position from the lowest menial to the important major-domo and the confidential secretary. Tiro was of this higher class. He had probably been born and brought up in the service, like Eliezer in the household of Abraham, and had become, like him, the trusted agent of his master and the friend of the whole family. He was evidently a person of considerable ability and accomplishments, acting as literary amanuensis, and indeed in some sort as a domestic critic, to his busy master. He had accompanied him to his government in Cilicia, and on the return home had been taken ill, and obliged to be left behind at Patrae. And this is Cicero's affectionate letter to him, written from Leucas (Santa Maura) the day afterwards:

"I thought I could have borne the separation from you better, but it is plainly impossible; and although it is of great importance to the honours which I am expecting[1] that I should get to Rome as soon as possible, yet I feel I made a great mistake in leaving you behind. But as it seemed to be your wish not to make the voyage until your health was restored, I approved your decision. Nor do I think otherwise now, if you are still of the same opinion. But if hereafter, when you are able to eat as usual, you think you can follow me here, it is for you to decide. I sent Mario to you, telling him either to join me with you as soon as possible, or, if you are delayed, to come back here at once. But be assured of this, that if it can be so without risk to your health, there is nothing I wish so much as to have you with me. Only, if you feel it necessary for your recovery to stay a little longer at Patrae, there is nothing I wish so much as for you to get well. If you sail at once, you will catch us at Leucas. But if you want to get well first, take care to secure pleasant companions, fine weather, and a good ship. Mind this, my good Tiro, if you love me—let neither Mario's visit nor this letter hurry you. By doing what is best for your own health, you will be best obeying my directions. Consider these points with your usual good sense. I miss you very much; but then I love you, and my affection makes me wish to see you well, just as my want of you makes me long to see you as soon as possible. But the first point is the most important. Above all, therefore, take care to get well: of all your innumerable services to me, this will be the most acceptable".

[Footnote 1: The triumph for the victory gained under his nominal command over the hill-tribes in Cilicia, during his governorship of that province (p. 68).]

Cicero writes to him continually during his own journey homewards with the most thoughtful kindness, begs that he will be cautious as to what vessel he sails in, and recommends specially one very careful captain. He has left a horse and a mule ready for him when he lands at Brundusium. Then he hears that Tiro had been foolish enough to go to a concert, or something of the kind, before he was strong, for which he mildly reproves him. He has written to the physician to spare no care or pains, and to charge, apparently, what he pleases. Several of his letters to his friend Atticus, at this date, speak in the most anxious and affectionate terms of the serious illness of this faithful servant. Just as he and his party are starting from Leucas, they send a note "from Cicero and his son, and Quintus the elder and younger, to their best and kindest Tiro". Then from Rome comes a letter in the name of the whole family, wife and daughter included:

"Marcus Tullius Cicero, and Cicero the younger, and Terentia, and Tullia, and Brother Quintus, and Quintus's Son, to Tiro send greeting.

"Although I miss your able and willing service every moment, still it is not on my own account so much as yours that I am sorry you are not well. But as your illness has now taken the form of a quartan fever (for so Curius writes), I hope, if you take care of yourself, you will soon be stronger. Only be sure, if you have any kindness for me, not to trouble yourself about anything else just now, except how to get well as soon as may be. I am quite aware how much you regret not being with me; but everything will go right if you get well. I would not have you hurry, or undergo the annoyance of sea-sickness while you are weak, or risk a sea-voyage in winter". Then he tells him all the news from Rome; how there had been quite an ovation on his arrival there; how Caesar was (he thought) growing dangerous to the state; and how his own coveted "triumph" was still postponed. "All this", he says, "I thought you would like to know". Then he concludes: "Over and over again, I beg you to take care to get well, and to send me a letter whenever you have an opportunity. Farewell, again and again".

Tiro got well, and outlived his kind master, who, very soon after this, presented him with his freedom. It is to him that we are said to be indebted for the preservation and publication of Cicero's correspondence. He wrote, also, a biography of him, which Plutarch had seen, and of which he probably made use in his own 'Life of Cicero', but which has not come down to us.

There was another of his household for whom Cicero had the same affection. This was Sositheus, also a slave, but a man, like Tiro, of some considerable education, whom he employed as his reader. His death affected Cicero quite as the loss of a friend. Indeed, his anxiety is such, that his Roman dignity is almost ashamed of it. "I grieve", he says, "more than I ought for a mere slave". Just as one might now apologise for making too much fuss about a favourite dog; for the slave was looked upon in scarcely a higher light in civilised Rome. They spoke of him in the neuter gender, as a chattel; and it was gravely discussed, in case of danger in a storm at sea, which it would be right first to cast overboard to lighten the ship, a valuable horse or an indifferent slave. Hortensius, the rival advocate who has been mentioned, a man of more luxurious habits and less kindly spirit than Cicero, who was said to feed the pet lampreys in his stews much better than he did his slaves, and to have shed tears at the death of one of these ugly favourites, would have probably laughed at Cicero's concern for Sositheus and Tiro.

But indeed every glimpse of this kind which Cicero's correspondence affords us gives token of a kindly heart, and makes us long to know something more. Some have suspected him of a want of filial affection, owing to a somewhat abrupt and curt announcement in a letter to Atticus of his father's death; and his stanch defenders propose to adopt, with Madvig, the reading, *discessit*—"left us", instead of *decessit*—"died". There really seems no occasion. Unless Atticus knew the father intimately, there was no need to dilate upon the old man's death; and Cicero mentions subsequently, in terms quite as brief, the marriage of his daughter and the birth of his son—events in which we are assured he felt deeply interested. If any further explanation of this seeming coldness be required, the following remarks of Mr. Forsyth are apposite and true:

"The truth is, that what we call *sentiment* was almost unknown to the ancient Romans, in whose writings it would be as vain to look for it as to look for traces of Gothic architecture amongst classic ruins. And this is something more than a mere illustration. It suggests a reason for the absence. Romance and sentiment came from the dark forests of the North, when Scandinavia and Germany poured forth their hordes to subdue and people the Roman Empire. The life of a citizen of the Republic of Rome was essentially a public life. The love of country was there carried to an extravagant length, and was paramount to, and almost swallowed up, the private and social affections. The state was everything, the individual comparatively nothing. In one of the letters of the Emperor Marcus Aurelius to Fronto, there is a passage in which he says that the Roman language had no word corresponding with the Greek [Greek: philostorgia], — the affectionate love for parents and children. Upon this Niebuhr remarks that the feeling was 'not a Roman one; but Cicero possessed it in a degree which few Romans could comprehend, and hence he was laughed at for the grief which he felt at the death of his daughter Tullia'".

CHAPTER X.

ESSAYS ON 'OLD AGE' AND 'FRIENDSHIP'

The treatise on 'Old Age', which is thrown into the form of a dialogue, is said to have been suggested by the opening of Plato's 'Republic', in which Cephalus touches so pleasantly on the enjoyments peculiar to that time of life. So far as light and graceful treatment of his subject goes, the Roman essayist at least does not fall short of his model. Montaigne said of it, that "it made one long to grow old"; [1] but Montaigne was a Frenchman, and such sentiment was quite in his way. The dialogue, whether it produce this effect on many readers or not, is very pleasant reading: and when we remember that the author wrote it when he was exactly in his grand climacteric, and addressed it to his friend Atticus, who was within a year of the same age, we get that element of personal interest which makes all writings of the kind more attractive. The argument in defence of the paradox that it is a good thing to grow old, proceeds upon the only possible ground, the theory of compensations. It is put into the mouth of Cato the Censor, who had died about a century before, and who is introduced as giving a kind of lecture on the subject to his young friends Scipio and Laelius, in his eighty-fourth year. He was certainly a remarkable example in his own case of its being possible to grow old gracefully and usefully, if, as he tells us, he was at that age still able to take part in the debates in the Senate, was busy collecting materials for the early history of Rome, had quite lately begun the study of Greek, could enjoy a country dinner-party, and had been thinking of taking lessons in playing on the lyre.

[Footnote 1: "Il donne l'appetit de vieiller".]

He states four reasons why old age is so commonly considered miserable. First, it unfits us for active employment; secondly, it weakens the bodily strength; thirdly, it deprives us of nearly all pleasures; fourthly and lastly, it is drawing near death. As to the first, the old senator argues very fairly that very much of the more important business of life is not only transacted by old men, but in point of fact, as is confessed by the very name and composition of the Roman Senate, it is thought safest to intrust it to the elders in the state. The pilot at the helm may not be able to climb the mast and run up and down the deck like the younger sailor, but he steers none the worse for being old. He quotes some well-known examples of this from Roman annals; examples which might be matched by obvious instances in modern English history. The defence which he makes of old age against the second charge—loss of muscular vigour—is rather more of the nature of special pleading. He says little more than that mere muscular strength, after all, is not much wanted for our happiness: that there are always comparative degrees of strength; and that an old man need no more make himself unhappy because he has not the strength of a young man, than the latter does because he has not the strength of a bull or an elephant. It was very well for the great wrestler Milo to be able to carry an ox round the arena on his shoulders; but, on the whole, a man does not often want to walk about with a bullock on his back. The old are said, too, to lose their memory. Cato thinks they can remember pretty well all that they care to remember. They are not apt to forget who owes them money; and "I never knew an old man forget", he says, "where he had buried his gold". Then as to the pleasures of the senses, which age undoubtedly diminishes our power of enjoying. "This", says Cato, "is really a privilege, not a deprivation; to be delivered from the yoke of such tyrants as our passions—to feel that we have 'got our discharge' from such a warfare—is a blessing for which men ought rather to be grateful to their advancing years". And the respect and authority which is by general consent conceded to old age, is a pleasure more than equivalent to the vanished pleasures of youth.

There is one consideration which the author has not placed amongst his four chief disadvantages of growing old, —which, however, he did not forget, for he notices it incidentally in the dialogue, —the feeling that we are growing less agreeable to our friends, that our company is less sought after, and that we are, in short, becoming rather ciphers in society. This, in a condition of high civilisation, is really perhaps felt by most of us as the hardest to bear of all the ills to which old age is liable. We should not care so much about the younger generation rising up and making us look old, if we did not feel that they are "pushing us from our stools". Cato admits that he had heard some old men complain that "they were now neglected by those who had once courted their society", and he quotes a passage from the comic poet Caecilius

"This is the bitterest pang in growing old, —
To feel that we grow hateful to our fellows".

But he dismisses the question briefly in his own case by observing with some complacency that he does not think his young friends find *his* company disagreeable—an assertion which Scipio and Laelius, who occasionally take part in the dialogue, are far too well bred to contradict. He remarks also, sensibly enough, that though some old persons are no doubt considered disagreeable company, this is in great measure their own fault: that testiness and ill-nature (qualities which, as he observes, do not usually improve with age) are always disagreeable, and that such persons attributed to their advancing years what was in truth the consequence of their unamiable tempers. It is not all wine which turns sour with age, nor yet all tempers; much depends on the original quality. The old Censor lays down some maxims which, like the preceding, have served as texts for a good many modern writers, and may be found expanded, diluted, or strengthened, in the essays of Addison and Johnson, and in many of their followers of less repute. "I never could assent", says Cato, "to that ancient and much-bepraised proverb, —that 'you must become an old man early, if you wish to be an old man long'". Yet it was a maxim which was very much acted upon by modern Englishmen a generation or two back. It was then thought almost a moral duty to retire into old age, and to assume all its disabilities as well as its privileges, after sixty years or even earlier. At present the world sides with Cato, and rushes perhaps into the other extreme; for any line at which old age now begins would be hard to trace either in dress or deportment. "We must resist old age, and fight against it as a disease". Strong words from the old Roman; but, undoubtedly, so long as we stop short of the attempt to affect juvenility, Cato is right. We should keep ourselves as young as possible. He speaks shrewd sense, again, when he says—"As I like to see a young man who has something old about him, so I like to see an old man in whom there remains something of the youth: and he who follows this maxim may become an old man in body, but never in heart". "What a blessing it is", says Southey, "to have a boy's heart! " Do we not all know these charming old people, to whom the young take almost as heartily as to their own equals in age, who are the favourite consultees in all amusements, the confidants in all troubles?

Cato is made to place a great part of his own enjoyment, in these latter years of his, in the cultivation of his farm and garden (he had written, we must remember, a treatise 'De Re Rustica', —a kind of Roman 'Book of the Farm', which we have still remaining). He is enthusiastic in his description of the pleasures of a country gentleman's life, and, like a good farmer, as no doubt he was, becomes eloquent upon the grand subject of manures. Gardening is a pursuit which he holds in equal honour—that "purest of human pleasures", as Bacon calls it. On the subject of the country life generally he confesses an inclination to become garrulous—the one failing which he admits may be fairly laid to the charge of old age. The picture of the way of living of a Roman gentleman-farmer, as he draws it, must have presented a strong contrast with the artificial city-life of Rome.

"Where the master of the house is a good and careful manager, his wine-cellar, his oil-stores, his larder, are always well stocked; there is a fulness throughout the whole establishment; pigs, kids, lambs, poultry, milk, cheese, honey, —all are in abundance. The produce of the garden is always equal, as our country-folk say, to a double course. And all these good things acquire a second relish from the voluntary labours of fowling and the chase. What need to dwell upon the charm of the green fields, the well-ordered plantations, the beauty of the vineyards and olive-groves? In short, nothing can be more luxuriant in produce, or more delightful to the eye, than a well-cultivated estate; and, to the enjoyment of this, old age is so far from being any hindrance, that it rather invites and allures us to such pursuits".

He has no patience with what has been called the despondency of old age—the feeling, natural enough at that time of life, but not desirable to be encouraged, that there is no longer any room for hope or promise in the future which gives so much of its interest to the present. He will not listen to the poet when he says again—

"He plants the tree that shall not see the fruit"

The answer which he would make has been often put into other and more elaborate language, but has a simple grandeur of its own. "If any should ask the aged cultivator for whom he plants, let him not hesitate to make this reply, —'For the immortal gods, who, as they willed me to inherit these possessions from my forefathers, so would have me hand them on to those that shall come after'".

The old Roman had not the horror of country society which so many civilised Englishmen either have or affect. "I like a talk", he says, "over a cup of wine". "Even when I am down at my Sabine estate, I daily make one at a party of my country neighbours, and we prolong our conversation very frequently far into the night". The words are put into Cato's mouth, but the voice is the well-known voice of Cicero. We find him here, as in his letters, persuading himself into the belief that the secret of happiness is to be found in the retirement of the country. And his genial and social nature beams through it all. We are reminded of his half-serious complaints to Atticus of his importunate visitors at Formiae, the dinner-parties which he was, as we say now, "obliged to go to", and which he so evidently enjoyed. [1]

[Footnote 1: "A clergyman was complaining of the want of society in the country where he lived, and said, 'They talk of *runts'* (i. e., young cows). 'Sir', said Mr. Salusbury, 'Mr. Johnson would learn to talk of runts; ' meaning that I was a man who would make the most of my situation, whatever it was". —Boswell's Life. Cicero was like Dr. Johnson.]

He is careful, however, to remind his readers that old age, to be really either happy or venerable, must not be the old age of the mere voluptuary or the debauchee; that the grey head, in order to be, even in his pagan sense, "a crown of glory", must have been "found in the way of righteousness". Shakespeare might have learned from Cicero in these points the moral which he puts into the mouth of his Adam—

"Therefore mine age is as a lusty winter,
Frosty but kindly".

It is a miserable old age, says the Roman, which is obliged to appeal to its grey hairs as its only claim to the respect of its juniors. "Neither hoar hairs nor wrinkles can arrogate reverence as their right. It is the life whose opening years have been honourably spent which reaps the reward of reverence at its close".

In discussing the last of the evils which accompany old age, the near approach of death, Cicero rises to something higher than his usual level. His Cato will not have death to be an evil at all; it is to him the escaping from "the prison of the body", —the "getting the sight of land at last after a long voyage, and coming into port". Nay, he does not admit that death is death. "I have never been able to persuade myself"; he says, quoting the words of Cyrus in Xenophon, "that our spirits were alive while they were in these mortal bodies, and died only when they departed out of them; or that the spirit then only becomes void of sense when it escapes from a senseless body; but that rather when freed from all admixture of corporality, it is pure and uncontaminated, then it most truly has sense". "I am fully persuaded", he says to his young listeners, "that your two fathers, my old and dearly-loved friends, are living now, and living that life which only is worthy to be so called". And he winds up the dialogue with the very beautiful apostrophe, one of the last utterances of the philosopher's heart, well known, yet not too well known to be here quoted:

"It likes me not to mourn over departing life, as many men, and men of learning, have done. Nor can I regret that I have lived, since I have so lived that I may trust I was not born in vain; and I depart out of life as out of a temporary lodging, not as out of my home. For nature has given it to us as an inn to tarry at by the way, not as a place to abide in. O glorious day! when I shall set out to join that blessed company and assembly of disembodied spirits, and quit this crowd and rabble of life! For I shall go my way, not only to those great men of whom I spoke, but to my own son Cato, than whom was never better man born, nor more full of dutiful affection; whose body I laid on the funeral pile—an office he should rather have done for me. [1] But his spirit has never left me; it still looks fondly back upon me, though it has gone assuredly into those abodes where he knew that I myself should follow. And this my great loss I seemed to bear with calmness; not that I bore it undisturbed, but that I still consoled myself with the thought that the separation between us could not be for long. And if I err in this—in that I believe the spirits of men to be immortal—I err willingly; nor would I have this mistaken belief of mine uprooted so long as I shall live. But if, after I am dead, I shall have no consciousness, as some curious philosophers assert, then I am not afraid of dead philosophers laughing at my mistake".

[Footnote 1: Burke touches the same key in speaking of his son; "I live in an inverted order. They who ought to have succeeded me have gone before me: they who should have been to me as posterity are in the place of ancestors".]

* * * * *

The essay on 'Friendship' is dedicated by the author to Atticus—an appropriate recognition, as he says, of the long and intimate friendship which had existed between themselves. It is thrown, like the other, into the form of a dialogue. The principal speaker here is one of the listeners in the former case—Laelius, surnamed the Wise—who is introduced as receiving a visit from his two sons-in-law, Fannius and Scaevola (the great lawyer before mentioned), soon after the sudden death of his great friend, the younger Scipio Africanus. Laelius takes the occasion, at the request of the young men, to give them his views and opinions on the subject of Friendship generally. This essay is perhaps more original than that upon 'Old Age', but certainly is not so attractive to a modern reader. Its great merit is the grace and polish of the language; but the arguments brought forward to prove what an excellent thing it is for a man to have good friends, and plenty of them, in this world, and the rules for his behaviour towards them, seem to us somewhat trite and commonplace, whatever might have been their effect upon a Roman reader.

Cicero is indebted to the Greek philosophers for the main outlines of his theory of friendship, though his acquaintance with the works of Plato and Aristotle was probably exceedingly superficial. He holds, with them, that man is a social animal; that "we are so constituted by nature that there must be some degree of association between us all, growing closer in proportion as we are brought into more intimate relations one with another". So that the social bond is a matter of instinct, not of calculation; not a cold commercial contract of profit and loss, of giving and receiving, but the fulfilment of one of the yearnings of our nature. Here he is in full accordance with the teaching of Aristotle, who, of all the various kinds of friendship to which he allows the common name, pronounces that which is founded merely upon interest—upon mutual interchange, by tacit agreement, of certain benefits—to be the least worthy of such a designation. Friendship is defined by Cicero to be "the perfect accord upon all questions, religious and social, together with mutual goodwill and affection". This "perfect accord", it must be confessed, is a very large requirement. He follows his Greek masters again in holding that true friendship can exist only amongst the good; that, in fact, all friendship must assume that there is something good and lovable in the person towards whom the feeling is entertained it may occasionally be a mistaken assumption; the good quality we think we see in our friend may have no existence save in our own partial imagination; but the existence of the counterfeit is an incontestable evidence of the true original. And the greatest attraction, and therefore the truest friendships, will always be of the good towards the good.

He admits, however, the notorious fact, that good persons are sometimes disagreeable; and he confesses that we have a right to seek in our friends amiability as well as moral excellence.

"Sweetness", he says—anticipating, as all these ancients so provokingly do, some of our most modern popular philosophers— "sweetness, both in language and in manner, is a very powerful attraction in the formation of friendships". He is by no means of the same opinion as Sisyphus in Lord Lytton's 'Tale of Miletus'—

"Now, then, I know thou really art my friend, —
None but true friends choose such unpleasant words".

He admits that it is the office of a friend to tell unpleasant truths sometimes; but there should be a certain amount of this indispensable "sweetness" to temper the bitterness of the advice. There are some friends who are continually reminding you of what they have done for you—"a disgusting set of people verily they are", says our author. And there are others who are always thinking themselves slighted; "in which case there is generally something of which they are conscious in themselves, as laying them open to contemptuous treatment".

Cicero's own character displays itself in this short treatise. Here, as everywhere, he is the politician. He shows a true appreciation of the duties and the qualifications of a true friend; but his own thoughts are running upon political friendships. Just as when, in many of his letters, he talks about "all honest men", he means "our party"; so here, when he talks of friends, he cannot help showing that it was of the essence of friendship, in his view, to hold the same political opinions, and that one great use of friends was that a man should not be isolated, as he had sometimes feared he was, in his political course. When he puts forward the old instances of Coriolanus and Gracchus, and discusses the question whether their "friends" were or were not bound to aid them in their treasonable designs against the state, he was surely thinking of the factions of his own times, and the troublesome brotherhoods which had gathered round Catiline and Clodius. Be this as it may, the advice which he makes Laelius give to his younger relatives is good for all ages, modern or ancient: "There is nothing in this world more valuable than friendship". "Next to the immediate blessing and providence of Almighty God", Lord Clarendon was often heard to say, "I owe all the little I know, and the little good that is in me, to the friendships and conversation I have still been used to, of the most excellent men in their several kinds that lived in that age".

CHAPTER XI.

CICERO'S PHILOSOPHY.

'THE TRUE ENDS OF LIFE'. [1]

Philosophy was to the Roman what religion is to me. It professed to answer, so far as it might be answered Pilate's question, "What is truth? " or to teach men, as Cicero described it, "the knowledge of things human and divine". Hence the philosopher invests his subject with all attributes of dignity. To him Philosophy brings all blessings in her train. She is the guide of life, the medicine for his sorrows, "the fountain-head of all perfect eloquence—the mother of all good deeds and good words". He invokes with affectionate reverence the great name of Socrates—the sage who had "first drawn wisdom down from heaven".

[Footnote 1: 'De Finibus Bonorum et Malorum'.]

No man ever approached his subject more richly laden with philosophic lore than Cicero. Snatching every leisure moment that he could from a busy life, he devotes it to the study of the great minds of former ages. Indeed, he held this study to be the duty of the perfect orator; a knowledge of the human mind was one of his essential qualifications. Nor could he conceive of real eloquence without it; for his definition of eloquence is, "wisdom speaking fluently". [1] But such studies were also suited to his own natural tastes. And as years passed on, and he grew weary of civil discords and was harassed by domestic troubles, the great orator turns his back upon the noisy city, and takes his parchments of Plato and Aristotle to be the friends of his councils and the companions of his solitude, seeking by their light to discover Truth, which Democritus had declared to be buried in the depths of the sea.

[Footnote 1: "Copiose loquens sapientia".]

Yet, after all, he professes to do little more than translate. So conscious is he that it is to Greece that Rome is indebted for all her literature, and so conscious, also, on the part of his countrymen, of what he terms "an arrogant disdain for everything national", that he apologises to his readers for writing for the million in their mother-tongue. Yet he is not content, as he says, to be "a mere interpreter".

He thought that by an eclectic process—adopting and rearranging such of the doctrines of his Greek masters as approved themselves to his own judgment—he might make his own work a substitute for theirs. His ambition is to achieve what he might well regard as the hardest of tasks—a popular treatise on philosophy; and he has certainly succeeded. He makes no pretence to originality; all he can do is, as he expresses it, "to array Plato in a Latin dress", and "present this stranger from beyond the seas with the freedom of his native, city". And so this treatise on the Ends of Life—a grave question even to the most careless thinker—is, from the nature of the case, both dramatic and rhetorical. Representatives of the two great schools of philosophy—the Stoics and Epicureans—plead and counter-plead in his pages, each in their turn; and their arguments are based on principles broad and universal enough to be valid even now. For now, as then, men are inevitably separated into two classes—amiable men of ease, who guide their conduct by the rudder-strings of pleasure—who for the most part "leave the world" (as has been finely said) "in the world's debt, having consumed much and produced nothing"; [1] or, on the other hand, zealous men of duty,

"Who scorn delights and live laborious days",

and act according to the dictates of their honour or their conscience. In practice, if not in theory, a man must be either Stoic or Epicurean.

[Footnote 1: Lord Derby.]

Each school, in this dialogue, is allowed to plead its own cause. "Listen" (says the Epicurean) "to the voice of nature that bids you pursue pleasure, and do not be misled by that vulgar conception of pleasure as mere sensual enjoyment; our opponents misrepresent us when they say that we advocate this as the highest good; we hold, on the contrary, that men often obtain the greatest pleasure by neglecting this baser kind. Your highest instances of martyrdom—of Decii devoting themselves for their country, of consuls putting their sons to death to preserve discipline—are not disinterested acts of sacrifice, but the choice of a present pain in order to procure a future pleasure. Vice is but ignorance of real enjoyment. Temperance alone can bring peace of mind; and the wicked, even if they escape public censure, 'are racked night and day by the anxieties sent upon them by the immortal gods'. We do not, in this, contradict your Stoic; we, too, affirm that only the wise man is really happy. Happiness is as impossible for a mind distracted by passions, as for a city divided by contending factions. The terrors of death haunt the guilty wretch, 'who finds out too late that he has devoted himself to money or power or glory to no purpose'. But the wise man's life is unalloyed happiness. Rejoicing in a clear conscience, 'he remembers the past with gratitude, enjoys the blessings of the present, and disregards the future'. Thus the moral to be drawn is that which Horace (himself, as he expresses it, 'one of the litter of Epicurus') impresses on his fair friend Leuconöe:

'Strain your wine, and prove your wisdom; life is short; should hope be more?
In the moment of our talking envious time has slipped away.
Seize the present, trust to-morrow e'en as little as you may'".

Passing on to the second book of the treatise, we hear the advocate of the counter-doctrine. Why, exclaims the Stoic, introduce Pleasure to the councils of Virtue? Why uphold a theory so dangerous in practice? Your Epicurean soon turns Epicure, and a class of men start up who have never seen the sun rise or set, who squander fortunes on cooks and perfumers, on costly plate and gorgeous rooms, and ransack sea and land for delicacies to supply their feasts. Epicurus gives his disciples a dangerous discretion in their choice. There is no harm in luxury (he tells us) provided it be free from inordinate desires. But who is to fix the limit to such vague concessions?

Nay, more, he degrades men to the level of the brute creation. In his view, there is nothing admirable beyond this pleasure—no sensation or emotion of the mind, no soundness or health of body. And what is this pleasure which he makes of such high account? How short-lived while it lasts! how ignoble when we recall it afterwards! But even the common feeling and sentiments of men condemn so selfish a doctrine. We are naturally led to uphold truth and abhor deceit, to admire Regulus in his tortures, and to despise a lifetime of inglorious ease. And then follows a passage which echoes the stirring lines of Scott—

"Sound, sound the clarion, fill the fife!
To all the sensual world proclaim,
One crowded hour of glorious life
Is worth an age without a name".

Do not then (concludes the Stoic) take good words in your mouth, and prate before applauding citizens of honour, duty, and so forth, while you make your private lives a mere selfish calculation of expediency. We were surely born for nobler ends than this, and none who is worthy the name of a man would subscribe to doctrines which destroy all honour and all chivalry. The heroes of old time won their immortality not by weighing pleasures and pains in the balance, but by being prodigal of their lives, doing and enduring all things for the sake of their fellow-men.

The opening scene in the third book is as lively and dramatic as (what was no doubt the writer's model) the introduction of a Platonic dialogue. Cicero has walked across from his Tusculan villa to borrow some manuscripts from the well-stocked library of his young friend Lucullus[1]—a youth whose high promise was sadly cut short, for he was killed at Philippi, when he was not more than twenty-three. There, "gorging himself with books", Cicero finds Marcus Cato—a Stoic of the Stoics—who expounds in a high tone the principles of his sect.

[Footnote 1: See p. 43.]

Honour he declares to be the rule, and "life according to nature" the end of man's existence. And wrong and injustice are more really contrary to this nature than either death, or poverty, or bodily suffering, or any other outward evil. [1] Stoics and Peripatetics are agreed at least on one point—that bodily pleasures fade into nothing before the splendours of virtue, and that to compare the two is like holding a candle against the sunlight, or setting a drop of brine against the waves of the ocean. Your Epicurean would have each man live in selfish isolation, engrossed in his private pleasures and pursuits. We, on the other hand, maintain that "Divine Providence has appointed the world to be a common city for men and gods", and each one of us to be a part of this vast social system. And thus every man has his lot and place in life, and should take for his guidance those golden rules of ancient times—"Obey God; know thyself; shun excess". Then, rising to enthusiasm, the philosopher concludes: "Who cannot but admire the incredible beauty of such a system of morality? What character in history or in fiction can be grander or more consistent than the 'wise man' of the Stoics? All the riches and glory of the world are his, for he alone can make a right use of all things. He is 'free', though he be bound by chains; 'rich', though in the midst of poverty; 'beautiful', for the mind is fairer than the body; 'a king', for, unlike the tyrants of the world, he is lord of himself; 'happy', for he has no need of Solon's warning to 'wait till the end', since a life virtuously spent is a perpetual happiness".

[Footnote 1: So Bishop Butler, in the preface to his Sermons upon 'Human Nature', says they were "intended to explain what is meant by the nature of man, when it is said that virtue consists in following, and vice in deviating from it".]

In the fourth book, Cicero himself proceeds to vindicate the wisdom of the ancients—the old Academic school of Socrates and his pupils—against what he considers the novelties of Stoicism. All that the Stoics have said has been said a hundred times before by Plato and Aristotle, but in nobler language. They merely "pick out the thorns" and "lay bare the bones" of previous systems, using newfangled terms and misty arguments with a "vainglorious parade". Their fine talk about citizens of the world and the ideal wise man is rather poetry than philosophy. They rightly connect happiness with virtue, and virtue with wisdom; but so did Aristotle some centuries before them.

But their great fault (says Cicero) is, that they ignore the practical side of life. So broad is the line which they draw between the "wise" and "foolish", that they would deny to Plato himself the possession of wisdom. They take no account of the thousand circumstances which go to form our happiness. To a spiritual being, virtue *might* be the chief good; but in actual life our physical is closely bound up with our mental enjoyment, and pain is one of those stern facts before which all theories are powerless. Again, by their fondness for paradox, they reduce all offences to the same dead level. It is, in their eyes, as impious to beat a slave as to beat a parent: because, as they say, "nothing can be *more* virtuous than virtue, —nothing *more* vicious than vice". And lastly, this stubbornness of opinion affects their personal character. They too often degenerate into austere critics and bitter partisans, and go far to banish from among us love, friendship, gratitude, and all the fair humanities of life.

The fifth book carries us back some twenty years, when we find Cicero once more at Athens, taking his afternoon walk among the deserted groves of the Academy. With him are his brother Quintus, his cousin Lucius, and his friends Piso and Atticus. The scene, with its historic associations, irresistibly carries their minds back to those illustrious spirits who had once made the place their own. Among these trees Plato himself had walked; under the shadow of that Porch Zeno had lectured to his disciples; [1] yonder Quintus points out the "white peak of Colonus", described by Sophocles in "those sweetest lines; " while glistening on the horizon were the waves of the Phaleric harbour, which Demosthenes, Cicero's own great prototype, had outvoiced with the thunder of his declamation. So countless, indeed, are the memories of the past called up by the genius of the place, that (as one of the friends remarks) "wherever we plant our feet, we tread upon some history". Then Piso, speaking at Cicero's request, begs his friends to turn from the degenerate thinkers of their own day to those giants of philosophy, from whose writings all liberal learning, all history, and all elegance of language may be derived. More than all, they should turn to the leader of the Peripatetics, Aristotle, who seemed (like Lord Bacon after him) to have taken all knowledge as his portion. From these, if from no other source, we may learn the secret of a happy life. But first we must settle what this 'chief good' is—this end and object of our efforts—and not be carried to and fro, like ships without a steersman, by every blast of doctrine.

[Footnote 1: The Stoics took their name from the 'stoa', or portico in the Academy, where they *sat* at lecture, as the Peripatetics (the school of Aristotle) from the little knot of listeners who followed their master as he *walked*. Epicurus's school were known as the philosophers of 'the Garden', from the place where he taught. The 'Old Academy' were the disciples of Plato; the 'New Academy' (to whose tenets Cicero inclined) revived the great principle of Socrates—of affirming nothing.]

If Epicurus was wrong in placing Happiness

"In corporal pleasure and in careless ease",

no less wrong are they who say that "honour" requires pleasure to be added to it, since they thus make honour itself dishonourable. And again, to say with others that happiness is tranquillity of mind, is simply to beg the question.

Putting, then, all such theories aside, we bring the argument to a practical issue. Self-preservation is the first great principle of nature; and so strong is this instinctive love of life both among men and animals, that we see even the iron-hearted Stoic shrink from the actual pangs of a voluntary death. Then comes the question, What *is* this nature that is so precious to each of us? Clearly it is compounded of body and mind, each with many virtues of its own; but as the mind should rule the body, so reason, as the dominant faculty, should rule the mind. Virtue itself is only "the perfection of this reason", and, call it what you will, genius or intellect is something divine.

Furthermore, there is in man a gradual progress of reason, growing with his growth until it has reached perfection. Even in the infant there are "as it were sparks of virtue"—half-unconscious principles of love and gratitude; and these germs bear fruit, as the child develops into the man. We have also an instinct which attracts us towards the pursuit of wisdom; such is the true meaning of the Sirens' voices in the Odyssey, says the philosopher, quoting from the poet of all time:

> "Turn thy swift keel and listen to our lay;
> Since never pilgrim to these regions came,
> But heard our sweet voice ere he sailed away,
> And in his joy passed on, with ampler mind". [1]

It is wisdom, not pleasure, which they offer. Hence it is that men devote their days and nights to literature, without a thought of any gain that may accrue from it; and philosophers paint the serene delights of a life of contemplation in the islands of the blest.

[Footnote 1: Odyss. xii. 185 (Worsley).]

Again, our minds can never rest. "Desire for action grows with us; " and in action of some sort, be it politics or science, life (if it is to be life at all) must be passed by each of us. Even the gambler must ply the dice-box, and the man of pleasure seek excitement in society. But in the true life of action, still the ruling principle should be honour.

Such, in brief, is Piso's (or rather Cicero's) vindication of the old masters of philosophy. Before they leave the place, Cicero fires a parting shot at the Stoic paradox that the 'wise man' is always happy. How. he pertinently asks, can one in sickness and poverty, blind, or childless, in exile or in torture, be possibly called happy, except by a monstrous perversion of language? [1]

[Footnote 1: In a little treatise called "Paradoxes", Cicero discusses six of these scholastic quibbles of the Stoics.]

Here, somewhat abruptly, the dialogue closes; and Cicero pronounces no judgment of his own, but leaves the great question almost as perplexed as when he started the discussion. But, of the two antagonistic theories, he leans rather to the Stoic than to the Epicurean. Self-sacrifice and honour seem, to his view, to present a higher ideal than pleasure or expediency.

II. 'ACADEMIC QUESTIONS'.

Fragments of two editions of this work have come down to us; for almost before the first copy had reached the hands of his friend Atticus, to whom it was sent, Cicero had rewritten the whole on an enlarged scale. The first book (as we have it now) is dedicated to Varro, a noble patron of art and literature. In his villa at Cumae were spacious porticoes and gardens, and a library with galleries and cabinets open to all comers. Here, on a terrace looking seawards, Cicero, Atticus, and Varro himself pass a long afternoon in discussing the relative merits of the old and new Academies; and hence we get the title of the work. Varro takes the lion's share of the first dialogue, and shows how from the "vast and varied genius of Plato" both Academics and Peripatetics drew all their philosophy, whether it related to morals, to nature, or to logic. Stoicism receives a passing notice, as also does what Varro considers the heresy of Theophrastus, who strips virtue of all its beauty, by denying that happiness depends upon it.

The second book is dedicated to another illustrious name, the elder Lucullus, not long deceased—half-statesman, half-dilettante, "with almost as divine a memory for facts", says Cicero, with something of envy, "as Hortensius had for words". This time it is at his villa, near Tusculum, amidst scenery perhaps even now the loveliest of all Italian landscapes, that the philosophic dialogue takes place. Lucullus condemns the scepticism of the New Academy—those reactionists against the dogmatism of past times, who disbelieve their very eyesight. If (he says) we reject the testimony of the senses, there is neither body, nor truth, nor argument, nor anything certain left us. These perpetual doubters destroy every ground of our belief.

Cicero ingeniously defends this scepticism, which was, in fact, the bent of his own mind. After all, what is our eyesight worth? The ship sailing across the bay yonder seems to move, but to the sailors it is the shore that recedes from their view. Even the sun, "which mathematicians affirm to be eighteen times larger than the earth, looks but a foot in diameter". And as it is with these things, so it is with all knowledge. Bold indeed must be the man who can define the point at which belief passes into certainty. Even the "fine frenzy" of the poet, his pictures of gods and heroes, are as lifelike to himself and to his hearers as though he actually saw them:

"See how Apollo, fair-haired god,
Draws in and bends his golden bow,
While on the left fair Dian waves her torch".

No—we are sure of nothing; and we are happy if, like Socrates, we only know this—that we know nothing. Then, as if in irony, or partly influenced perhaps by the advocate's love of arguing the case both ways, Cicero demolishes that grand argument of design which elsewhere he so carefully constructs, [1] and reasons in the very language of materialism—"You assert that all the universe could not have been so ingeniously made without some godlike wisdom, the majesty of which you trace down even to the perfection of bees and ants. Why, then, did the Deity, when he made everything for the sake of man, make such a variety (for instance) of venomous reptiles? Your divine soul is a fiction; it is better to imagine that creation is the result of the laws of nature, and so release the Deity from a great deal of hard work, and me from fear; for which of us, when he thinks that he is an object of divine care, can help feeling an awe of the divine power day and night? But we do not understand even our own bodies; how, then, can we have an eyesight so piercing as to penetrate the mysteries of heaven and earth? "

[Footnote 1: See p. 168.]

The treatise, however, is but a disappointing fragment, and the argument is incomplete.

III. THE 'TUSCULAN DISPUTATIONS'.

The scene of this dialogue is Cicero's villa at Tusculum. There, in his long gallery, he walks and discusses with his friends the vexed questions of morality. Was death an evil? Was the soul immortal? How could a man best bear pain and the other miseries of life? Was virtue any guarantee for happiness?

Then, as now, death was the great problem of humanity—"to die and go we know not where". The old belief in Elysium and Tartarus had died away; as Cicero himself boldly puts it in another place, such things were no longer even old wives' fables. Either death brought an absolute unconsciousness, or the soul soared into space. "*Lex non poena mors*"—"Death is a law, not a penalty"—was the ancient saying. It was, as it were, the close of a banquet or the fall of the curtain. "While we are, death is not; when death has come, we are not".

Cicero brings forward the testimony of past ages to prove that death is not a mere annihilation. Man cannot perish utterly. Heroes are deified; and the spirits of the dead return to us in visions of the night. Somehow or other (he says) there clings to our minds a certain presage of future ages; and so we plant, that our children may reap; we toil, that others may enter into our labours; and it is this life after death, the desire to live in men's mouths for ever, which inspires the patriot and the martyr. Fame to the Roman, even more than to us, was "the last infirmity of noble minds". It was so in a special degree to Cicero. The instinctive sense of immortality, he argues, is strong within us; and as, in the words of the English poet,

"Our birth is but a sleep and a forgetting",

so also in death, the Roman said, though in other words:

"Our souls have sight of that immortal sea
Which brought us hither".

Believe not then, says Cicero, those old wives' tales, those poetic legends, the terrors of a material hell, of the joys of a sensual paradise. Rather hold with Plato that the soul is an eternal principle of life, which has neither beginning nor end of existence; for if it were not so, heaven and earth would be overset, and all nature

109

would stand at gaze. "Men say they cannot conceive or comprehend what the soul can be, distinct from the body. As if, forsooth, they could comprehend what it is, when it is *in* the body, —its conformation, its magnitude, or its position there.... To me, when I consider the nature of the soul, there is far more difficulty and obscurity in forming a conception of what the soul is while in the body, —in a dwelling where it seems so little at home, —than of what it will be when it has escaped into the free atmosphere of heaven, which seems its natural abode". [1] And as the poet seems to us inspired, as the gifts of memory and eloquence seem divine, so is the soul itself, in its simple essence, a god dwelling in the breast of each of us. What else can be this power which enables us to recollect the past, to foresee the future, to understand the present?

[Footnote 1: I. c. 22.]

There follows a passage on the argument from design which anticipates that fine saying of Voltaire—"Si Dieu n'existait pas, il faudrait l'inventer; mais toute la nature crie qu'il existe". "The heavens", says even the heathen philosopher, "declare the glory of God". Look on the sun and the stars; look on the alternation of the seasons, and the changes of day and night; look again at the earth bringing forth her fruits for the use of men; the multitude of cattle; and man himself, made as it were to contemplate and adore the heavens and the gods. Look on all these things, and doubt not that there is some Being, though you see him not, who has created and presides over the world.

"Imitate, therefore, the end of Socrates; who, with the fatal cup in his hands, spoke with the serenity of one not forced to die, but, as it were, ascending into heaven; for he thought that the souls of men, when they left the body, went by different roads; those polluted by vice and unclean living took a road wide of that which led to the assembly of the gods; while those who had kept themselves pure, and on earth had taken a divine life as their model, found it easy to return to those beings from whence they came". Or learn a lesson from the swans, who, with a prophetic instinct, leave this world with joy and singing. Yet do not anticipate the time of death, "for the Deity forbids us to depart hence without his summons; but, on just cause given (as to Socrates and Cato), gladly should we exchange our darkness for that light, and, like men not breaking prison but released by the law, leave our chains with joy, as having been discharged by God".

The feeling of these ancients with regard to suicide, we must here remember, was very different from our own. There was no distinct idea of the sanctity of life; no social stigma and consequent suffering were brought on the family of the suicide. Stoic and Epicurean philosophers alike upheld it as a lawful remedy against the pangs of disease, the dotage of old age, or the caprices of a tyrant. Every man might, they contended, choose his own route on the last great journey, and sleep well, when he grew wearied out with life's fitful fever. The door was always open (said Epictetus) when the play palled on the senses. You should quit the stage with dignity, nor drain the flask to the dregs. Some philosophers, it is true, protested against it as a mere device of cowardice to avoid pain, and as a failure in our duties as good citizens. Cicero, in one of his latest works, again quotes with approval the opinion of Pythagoras, that "no man should abandon his post in life without the orders of the Great Commander". But at Rome suicide had been glorified by a long roll of illustrious names, and the protest was made in vain.

But why, continues Cicero, why add to the miseries of life by brooding over death? Is life to any of us such unmixed pleasure even while it lasts? Which of us can tell whether he be taken away from good or from evil? As our birth is but "a sleep and a forgetting", so our death may be but a second sleep, as lasting as Endymion's. Why then call it wretched, even if we die before our natural time? Nature has lent us life, without fixing the day of payment; and uncertainty is one of the conditions of its tenure. Compare our longest life with eternity, and it is as short-lived as that of those ephemeral insects whose life is measured by a summer day; and "who, when the sun sets, have reached old age".

Let us, then, base our happiness on strength of mind, on a contempt of earthly pleasures, and on the strict observance of virtue. Let us recall the last noble words of Socrates to his judges. "The death", said he, "to which you condemn me, I count a gain rather than a loss. Either it is a dreamless sleep that knows no waking, or it carries me where I may converse with the spirits of the illustrious dead. *I* go to death, *you* to life; but which of us is going the better way, God only knows".

No man, then, dies too soon who has run a course of perfect virtue; for glory follows like a shadow in the wake of such a life. Welcome death, therefore, as a blessed deliverance from evil, sent by the special favour of the gods, who thus bring us safely across a sea of troubles to an eternal haven.

The second topic which Cicero and his friends discuss is, the endurance of pain. Is it an unmixed evil? Can anything console the sufferer? Cicero at once condemns the sophistry of Epicurus. The wise man cannot pretend indifference to pain; it is enough that he endure it with courage, since, beyond all question, it is sharp, bitter, and hard to bear. And what is this courage? Partly excitement, partly the impulse of honour or of shame, partly the habituation which steels the endurance of the gladiator. Keep, therefore—this is the conclusion—stern restraint over the feminine elements of your soul, and learn not only to despise the attacks of pain, but also

> "The slings and arrows of outrageous fortune".

From physical, the discussion naturally passes to mental, suffering. For grief, as well as for pain, he prescribes the remedy of the Stoics—*aequanimitas*—"a calm serenity of mind". The wise man, ever serene and composed, is moved neither by pain or sorrow, by fear or desire. He is equally undisturbed by the malice of enemies or the inconstancy of fortune. But what consolation can we bring to ease the pain of the Epicurean? "Put a nosegay to his nostrils—burn perfumes before him—crown him with roses and woodbine"! But perfumes and garlands can do little in such case; pleasures may divert, but they can scarcely console.

Again, the Cyrenaics bring at the best but Job's comfort. No man will bear his misfortunes the more lightly by bethinking himself that they are unavoidable—that others have suffered before him—that pain is part and parcel of the ills which flesh is heir to. Why grieve at all? Why feed your misfortune by dwelling on it? Plunge rather into active life and forget it, remembering that excessive lamentation over the trivial accidents of humanity is alike unmanly and unnecessary. And as it is with grief, so it is with envy, lust, anger, and those other "perturbations of the mind" which the Stoic Zeno rightly declares to be "repugnant to reason and nature". From such disquietudes it is the wise man who is free.

The fifth and last book discusses the great question, Is virtue of itself sufficient to make life happy? The bold conclusion is, that it is sufficient. Cicero is not content with the timid qualifications adopted by the school of the Peripatetics, who say one moment that external advantages and worldly prosperity are nothing, and then again admit that, though man may be happy without them, he is happier with them, —which is making the real happiness imperfect after all. Men differ in their views of life. As in the great Olympic games, the throng are attracted, some by desire of gain, some by the crown of wild olive, some merely by the spectacle; so, in the race of life, we are all slaves to some ruling idea, it may be glory, or money, or wisdom. But they alone can be pronounced happy whose minds are like some tranquil sea—"alarmed by no fears, wasted by no griefs, inflamed by no lusts, enervated by no relaxing pleasures, —and such serenity virtue alone can produce".

These 'Disputations' have always been highly admired. But their popularity was greater in times when Cicero's Greek originals were less read or understood. Erasmus carried his admiration of this treatise to enthusiasm. "I cannot doubt", he says, "but that the mind from which such teaching flowed was inspired in some sort by divinity".

IV. THE TREATISE 'ON MORAL DUTIES'.

The treatise 'De Officiis', known as Cicero's 'Offices, to which we pass next, is addressed by the author to his son, while studying at Athens under Cratippus; possibly in imitation of Aristotle, who inscribed his Ethics to his son Nicomachus. It is a treatise on the duties of a gentleman—"the noblest present", says a modern writer, "ever made by parent to a child". [1] Written in a far higher tone than Lord Chesterfield's letters, though treating of the same subject, it proposes and answers multifarious questions which must occur continually to the modern Christian as well as to the ancient philosopher. "What makes an action right or wrong? What is a duty? What is expediency? How shall I learn to choose between my principles and my interests? And lastly (a point of casuistry which must sometimes perplex the strictest conscience), of two 'things honest', [2] which is most so? "

[Footnote 1: Kelsall.]

[Footnote 2: The English "Honesty" and "Honour" alike fail to convey the full force of the Latin *honestus*. The word expresses a progress of thought from comeliness and grace of person to a noble and graceful character—all whose works are done in honesty and honour.]

The key-note of his discourse throughout is Honour; and the word seems to carry with it that magic force which Burke attributed to chivalry—"the unbought grace of life—the nurse of heroic sentiment and manly enterprise". *Noblesse oblige,* —and there is no state of life, says Cicero, without its obligations. In their due discharge consists all the nobility, and in their neglect all the disgrace, of character. There should be no selfish devotion to private interests. We are born not for ourselves only, but for our kindred and fatherland. We owe duties not only to those who have benefited but to those who have wronged us. We should render to all their due; and justice is due even to the lowest of mankind: what, for instance (he says with a hardness which jars upon our better feelings), can be lower than a slave? Honour is that "unbought grace" which adds a lustre to every action. In society it produces courtesy of manners; in business, under the form of truth, it establishes public credit. Again, as equity, it smooths the harsh features of the law. In war it produces that moderation and good faith between contending armies which are the surest basis of a lasting peace. And so in honour are centred the elements of all the virtues—wisdom and justice, fortitude and temperance; and "if", he says, reproducing the noble words of Plato, as applied by him to Wisdom, "this 'Honour' could but be seen in her full beauty by mortal eyes, the whole world would fall in love with her".

Such is the general spirit of this treatise, of which only the briefest sketch can be given in these pages.

Cicero bases honour on our inherent excellence of nature, paying the same noble tribute to humanity as Kant some centuries after: "On earth there is nothing great but man; in man there is nothing great but mind". Truth is a law of our nature. Man is only "lower than the angels"; and to him belong prerogatives which mark him off from the brute creation—the faculties of reason and discernment, the sense of beauty, and the love of law and order. And from this arises that fellow—feeling which, in one sense, "makes the whole world kin"—the spirit of Terence's famous line, which Cicero notices (applauded on its recitation, as Augustin tells us, by the cheers of the entire audience in the theatre)—

"Homo sum—humani nihil a me alienum puto: " [1]

for (he continues) "all men by nature love one another, and desire an intercourse of words and action". Hence spring the family affections, friendship, and social ties; hence also that general love of combination, which forms a striking feature of the present age, resulting in clubs, trades-unions, companies, and generally in what Mr. Carlyle terms "swarmery".

[Footnote 1: "I am a man—I hold that nothing which concerns mankind can be matter of unconcern to me".]

Next to truth, justice is the great duty of mankind. Cicero at once condemns "communism" in matters of property. Ancient immemorial seizure, conquest, or compact, may give a title; but "no man can say that he has anything his own by a right of nature". Injustice springs from avarice or ambition, the thirst of riches or of empire, and is the more dangerous as it appears in the more exalted spirits, causing a dissolution of all ties and obligations. And here he takes occasion to instance "that late most shameless attempt of Caesar's to make himself master of Rome".

There is, besides, an injustice of omission. You may wrong your neighbour by seeing him wronged without interfering. Cicero takes the opportunity of protesting strongly against the selfish policy of those lovers of ease and peace, who, "from a desire of furthering their own interests, or else from a churlish temper, profess that they mind nobody's business but their own, in order that they may seem to be men of strict integrity and to injure none", and thus shrink from taking their part in "the fellowship of life". He would have had small patience with our modern doctrine of non-intervention and neutrality in nations any more than in men. Such conduct arises (he says) from the false logic with which men cheat their conscience; arguing reversely, that whatever is the best policy is—honesty.

There are two ways, it must be remembered, in which one man may injure another—force and fraud; but as the lion is a nobler creature than the fox, so open violence seems less odious than secret villany. No character is so justly hateful as

> "A rogue in grain,
> Veneered with sanctimonious theory".

Nations have their obligations as well as individuals, and war has its laws as well as peace. The struggle should be carried on in a generous temper, and not in the spirit of extermination, when "it has sometimes seemed a question between two hostile nations, not which should remain a conqueror, but which should remain a nation at all".

No mean part of justice consists in liberality, and this, too, has its duties. It is an important question, how, and when, and to whom, we should give? It is possible to be generous at another person's expense: it is possible to injure the recipient by mistimed liberality; or to ruin one's fortune by open house and prodigal hospitality. A great man's bounty (as he says in another place) should be a common sanctuary for the needy. "To ransom captives and enrich the meaner folk is a nobler form of generosity than providing wild beasts or shows of gladiators to amuse the mob". Charity should begin at home; for relations and friends hold the first place in our affections; but the circle of our good deeds is not to be narrowed by the ties of blood, or sect, or party, and "our country comprehends the endearments of all". We should act in the spirit of the ancient law— "Thou shalt keep no man from the running stream, or from lighting his torch at thy hearth". Our liberality should be really liberal, —like that charity which Jeremy Taylor describes as "friendship to all the world".

Another component principle of this honour is courage, or "greatness of soul", which (continues Cicero) has been well defined by the Stoics as "a virtue contending for justice and honesty"; and its noblest form is a generous contempt for ordinary objects of ambition, not "from a vain or fantastic humour, but from solid principles of reason". The lowest and commoner form of courage is the mere animal virtue of the fighting-cock.

But a character should not only be excellent, —it should be graceful. In gesture and deportment men should strive to acquire that dignified grace of manners "which adds as it were a lustre to our lives". They should avoid affectation and eccentricity; "not to care a farthing what people think of us is a sign not so much of pride as of immodesty". The want of tact—the saying and doing things at the wrong time and place—produces the same discord in society as a false note in music; and harmony of character is of more consequence than harmony of sounds. There is a grace in words as well as in conduct: we should avoid unseasonable jests, "and not lard our talk with Greek quotations". [1]

[Footnote 1: This last precept Cicero must have considered did not apply to letter-writing, otherwise he was a notorious offender against his own rule.]

In the path of life, each should follow the bent of his own genius, so far as it is innocent—

> "Honour and shame from no condition rise;
> Act well your part—there all the honour lies".

Nothing is so difficult (says Cicero) as the choice of a profession, inasmuch as "the choice has commonly to be made when the judgment is weakest". Some tread in their father's steps, others beat out a fresh line of their own; and (he adds, perhaps not without a personal reference) this is generally the case with those born of mean parents, who propose to carve their own way in the world. But the *parvenu* of Arpinum—the 'new man', as aristocratic jealousy always loved to call him—is by no means insensible to the true honours of ancestry. "The noblest inheritance", he says, "that can ever be left by a father to his son, far excelling that of lands and houses, is the fame of his virtues and glorious actions"; and saddest of all sights is that of a noble house dragged through the mire by some degenerate descendant, so as to be a by-word among the populace, —"which may" (he concludes) "be justly said of but too many in our times".

The Roman's view of the comparative dignity of professions and occupations is interesting, because his prejudices (if they be prejudices) have so long maintained their ground amongst us moderns. Tax-gatherers and usurers are as unpopular now as ever— the latter very deservedly so. Retail trade is despicable, we are told, and "all mechanics are by their profession mean". Especially such trades as minister to mere appetite or luxury—butchers, fishmongers, and cooks; perfumers, dancers, and suchlike. But medicine, architecture, education, farming, and even wholesale business, especially importation and exportation, are the professions of a gentleman. "But if the merchant, satisfied with his profits, shall leave the seas and from the harbour step into a landed estate, such a man seems justly deserving of praise". We seem to be reading the verdict of modern English society delivered by anticipation two thousand years ago.

The section ends with earnest advice to all, that they should put their principles into practice. "The deepest knowledge of nature is but a poor and imperfect business", unless it proceeds into action. As justice consists in no abstract theory, but in upholding society among men, —as "greatness of soul itself, if it be isolated from the duties of social life, is but a kind of uncouth churlishness", —so it is each citizen's duty to leave his philosophic seclusion of a cloister, and take his place in public life, if the times demand it, "though he be able to number the stars and measure out the world".

The same practical vein is continued in the next book. What, after all, are a man's real interests? what line of conduct will best advance the main end of his life? Generally, men make the fatal mistake of assuming that honour must always clash with their interests, while in reality, says Cicero, "they would obtain their ends best, not by knavery and underhand dealing, but by justice and integrity". The right is identical with the expedient. "The way to secure the favour of the gods is by upright dealing; and next to the gods, nothing contributes so much to men's happiness as men themselves". It is labour and co-operation which have given us all the goods which we possess.

Since, then, man is the best friend to man, and also his most formidable enemy, an important question to be discussed is the secret of influence and popularity—the art of winning men's affections. For to govern by bribes or by force is not really to govern at all; and no obedience based on fear can be lasting—"no force of power can bear up long against a current of public hate". Adventurers who ride rough-shod over law (he is thinking again of Caesar) have but a short-lived reign; and "liberty, when she has been chained up a while, bites harder when let loose than if she had never been chained at all". [1] Most happy was that just and moderate government of Rome in earlier times, when she was "the port and refuge for princes and nations in their hour of need". Three requisites go to form that popular character which has a just influence over others; we must win men's love, we must deserve their confidence, and we must inspire them with an admiration for our abilities. The shortest and most direct road to real influence is that which Socrates recommends—"for a man to be that which he wishes men to take him for". [2]

[Footnote 1: It is curious to note how, throughout the whole of this argument, Cicero, whether consciously or unconsciously, works upon the principle that the highest life is the political life, and that the highest object a man can set before him is the obtaining, by legitimate means, influence and authority amongst his fellow-citizens.]

[Footnote 2:

"Not being less but more than all
The gentleness he seemed to be".
—Tennyson: 'In Memoriam'.]

Then follow some maxims which show how thoroughly conservative was the policy of our philosopher. The security of property he holds to be the security of the state. There must be no playing with vested rights, no unequal taxation, no attempt to bring all things to a level, no cancelling of debts and redistribution of land (he is thinking of the baits held out by Catiline), none of those traditional devices for winning favour with the people, which tend to destroy that social concord and unity which make a common wealth. "What reason is there", he asks, "why, when I have bought, built, repaired, and laid out much money, another shall come and enjoy the fruits of it? "

And as a man should be careful of the interests of the social body, so he should be of his own. But Cicero feels that in descending to such questions he is somewhat losing sight of his dignity as a moralist. "You will find all this thoroughly discussed", he says to his son, "in Xenophon's Economics—a book which, when I was just your age, I translated from the Greek into Latin". [One wonders whether young Marcus took the hint.] "And if you want instruction in money matters, there are gentlemen sitting on the Exchange who will teach you much better than the philosophers".

The last book opens with a saying of the elder Cato's, which Cicero much admires, though he says modestly that he was never able in his own case quite to realise it—"I am never less idle than when I am idle, and never less alone than when alone". Retirement and solitude are excellent things, Cicero always declares; generally contriving at the same time to make it plain, as he does here, that his own heart is in the world of public life. But at least it gives him time for writing. He "has written more in this short time, since the fall of the Commonwealth, than in all the years during which it stood".

He here resolves the question, If honour and interest seem to clash, which is to give way? Or rather, it has been resolved already; if the right be always the expedient, the opposition is seeming, not real. He puts a great many questions of casuistry, but it all amounts to this: the good man keeps his oath, "though it were to his own hindrance". But it is never to his hindrance; for a violation of his conscience would be the greatest hindrance of all.

In this treatise, more than in any of his other philosophical works, Cicero inclines to the teaching of the Stoics. In the others, he is rather the seeker after truth than the maintainer of a system. His is the critical eclecticism of the 'New Academy'—the spirit so prevalent in our own day, which fights against the shackles of dogmatism. And with all his respect for the nobler side of Stoicism, he is fully alive to its defects; though it was not given to him to see, as Milton saw after him, the point wherein that great system really failed—the "philosophic pride" which was the besetting sin of all disciples in the school, from Cato to Seneca:

"Ignorant of themselves, of God much more,

* * * * *

Much of the soul they talk, but all awry;
And in themselves seek virtue, and to themselves
All glory arrogate, —to God give none;
Rather accuse Him under usual names,
Fortune, or Fate, as one regardless quite
Of mortal things". [1]

[Footnote 1: Paradise Regained.]

Yet, in spite of this, such men were as the salt of the earth in a corrupt age; and as we find, throughout the more modern pages of history, great preachers denouncing wickedness in high places, — Bourdaloue and Massillon pouring their eloquence into the heedless ears of Louis XIV, and his courtiers—Sherlock and Tillotson declaiming from the pulpit in such stirring accents that "even the indolent Charles roused himself to listen, and the fastidious Buckingham forgot to sneer"[1]—so, too, do we find these "monks of heathendom", as the Stoics have been not unfairly called, protesting in their day against that selfish profligacy which was fast sapping all morality in the Roman empire. No doubt (as Mr. Lecky takes care to tell us), their high principles were not always consistent with their practice (alas! whose are?); Cato may have ill-used his slaves, Sallust may have been rapacious, and Seneca wanting in personal courage. Yet it was surely something to have set up a noble ideal, though they might not attain to it themselves, and in "that hideous carnival of vice" to have kept themselves, so far as they might, unspotted from the world. Certain it is that no other ancient sect ever came so near the light of revelation. Passages from Seneca, from Epictetus, from Marcus Aurelius, sound even now like fragments of the inspired writings. The Unknown God, whom they ignorantly worshipped as the Soul or Reason of the World, is—in spite of Milton's strictures— the beginning and the end of their philosophy. Let us listen for a moment to their language. "Prayer should be only for the good". "Men should act according to the spirit, and not according to the letter of their faith". "Wouldest thou propitiate the gods? Be good: he has worshipped them sufficiently who has imitated them". It was from a Stoic poet, Aratus, that St. Paul quoted the great truth which was the rational argument against idolatry—"For we are also His offspring, and" (so the original passage concludes) "we alone possess a voice, which is the image of reason". It is in another poet of the same school that we find what are perhaps the noblest lines in all Latin poetry. Persius concludes his Satire on the common hypocrisy of those prayers and offerings to the gods which were but a service of the lips and hands, in words of which an English rendering may give the sense but not the beauty: "Nay, then, let us offer to the gods that which the debauched sons of great Messala can never bring on their broad chargers, —a soul wherein the laws of God and man are blended, —a heart pure to its inmost depths, —a breast ingrained with a noble sense of honour. Let me but bring these with me to the altar, and I care not though my offering be a handful of corn". With these grand words, fit precursors of a purer creed to come, we may take our leave of the Stoics, remarking how thoroughly, even in their majestic egotism, they represented the moral force of the nation among whom they flourished; a nation, says a modern preacher, "whose legendary and historic heroes could thrust their hand into the flame, and see it consumed without a nerve shrinking; or come from captivity on parole, advise their countrymen against a peace, and then go back to torture and certain death; or devote themselves by solemn self-sacrifice like the Decii. The world must bow before such men; for, unconsciously, here was a form of the spirit of the Cross-self-surrender, unconquerable fidelity to duty, sacrifice for others". [2]

[Footnote 1: Macaulay.]

[Footnote 2: F. W. Robertson, Sermons, i. 218.]

Portions of three treatises by Cicero upon Political Philosophy have come down to us: 1. I De Republica'; a dialogue on Government, founded chiefly on the 'Republic' of Plato: 2. 'De Legibus'; a discussion on Law in the abstract, and on national systems of legislation 3. 'De Jure Civili'; of which last only a few fragments exist. His historical works have all perished.

CHAPTER XII.

CICERO'S RELIGION.

It is difficult to separate Cicero's religion from his philosophy. In both he was a sceptic, but in the better sense of the word. His search after truth was in no sneering or incredulous spirit, but in that of a reverent inquirer. We must remember, in justice to him, that an earnest-minded man in his day could hardly take higher ground than that of the sceptic. The old polytheism was dying out in everything but in name, and there was nothing to take its place.

His religious belief, so far as we can gather it, was rather negative than positive. In the speculative treatise which he has left us, 'On the Nature of the Gods', he examines all the current creeds of the day, but leaves his own quite undefined.

The treatise takes the form, like the rest, of an imaginary conversation. This is supposed to have taken place at the house of Aurelius Cotta, then Pontifex Maximus—an office which answered nearly to that of Minister of religion. The other speakers are Balbus, Velleius, and Cicero himself, —who acts, however, rather in the character of moderator than of disputant. The debate is still, as in the more strictly philosophical dialogues, between the different schools. Velleius first sets forth the doctrine of his master Epicurus; speaking about the gods, says one of his opponents, with as much apparent intimate knowledge "as if he had just come straight down from heaven". All the speculations of previous philosophers—which he reviews one after the other—are, he assures the company, palpable errors. The popular mythology is a mere collection of fables. Plato and the Stoics, with their Soul of the world and their pervading Providence, are entirely wrong; the disciples of Epicurus alone are right. There are gods; that much, the universal belief of mankind in all ages sufficiently establishes. But that they should be the laborious beings which the common systems of theology would make them, — that they should employ themselves in the manufacture of worlds, —is manifestly absurd. Some of this argument is ingenious. "What should induce the Deity to perform the functions of an Aedile, to light up and decorate the world? If it was to supply better accommodation for himself, then he must have dwelt of choice, up to that time, in the darkness of a dungeon. If such improvements gave him pleasure, why should he have chosen to be without them so long? "

No—the gods are immortal and happy beings; and these very attributes imply that they should be wholly free from the cares of business—exempt from labour, as from pain and death. They are in human form, but of an ethereal and subtile essence, incapable of our passions or desires. Happy in their own perfect wisdom and virtue, they

"Sit beside their nectar, careless of mankind".

Cotta—speaking in behalf of the New Academy—controverts these views. Be these your gods, Epicurus, as well say there are no gods at all. What reverence, what love, or what fear can men have of beings who neither wish them, nor can work them, good or ill? Is idleness the divinest life? "Why, 'tis the very heaven of schoolboys; yet the schoolboys, on their holiday, employ themselves in games". Nay, he concludes, what the Stoic Posidonius said of your master Epicurus is true—"He believed there were no gods, and what he said about their nature he said only to avoid popular odium". He could not believe that the Deity has the outward shape of a man, without any solid essence; that he has all the members of a man, without the power to use them; that he is a shadowy transparent being, who shows no favour and confers no benefits on any, cares for nothing and does nothing; this is to allow his existence of the gods in word, but to deny it in fact.

Velleius compliments his opponent on his clever argument, but desires that Balbus would state his views upon the question. The Stoic consents; and, at some length, proceeds to prove (what neither disputant has at all denied) the existence of Divine beings of some kind. Universal belief, well-authenticated instances of their appearance to men, and of the fulfilment of prophecies and omens, are all evidences of their existence. He dwells much, too, on the argument from design, of which so much use has been made by modern theologians. He furnishes Paley with the idea for his well-known illustration of the man who finds a watch; "when we see a dial or a water-clock, we believe that the hour is shown thereon by art, and not by chance". [1] He gives also an illustration from the poet Attius, which from a poetical imagination has since become an historical incident; the shepherds who see the ship Argo approaching take the new monster for a thing of life, as the Mexicans regarded the ships of Cortes. Much more, he argues, does the harmonious order of the world bespeak an intelligence within. But his conclusion is that the Universe itself is the Deity; or that the Deity is the animating Spirit of the Universe; and that the popular mythology, which gives one god to the Earth, one to the Sea, one to Fire, and so on, is in fact a distorted version of this truth. The very form of the universe—the sphere—is the most perfect of all forms, and therefore suited to embody the Divine.

[Footnote 1: De Nat. Deor. ii. 34. Paley's Nat. Theol. ch. i.]

Then Cotta—who though, as Pontifex, he is a national priest by vocation, is of that sect in philosophy which makes doubt its creed—resumes his objections. He is no better satisfied with the tenets of the Stoics than with those of the Epicureans. He believes that there are gods; but, coming to the discussion as a dispassionate and philosophical observer, he finds such proofs as are offered of their existence insufficient. But this third book is fragmentary, and the continuity of Cotta's argument is broken by considerable gaps in all the manuscripts. There is a curious tradition, that these portions were carefully torn out by the early Christians, because they might prove too formidable weapons in the hands of unbelievers. Cotta professes throughout only to raise his objections in the hope that they may be refuted; but his whole reasoning is destructive of any belief in an overruling Providence. He confesses himself puzzled by that insoluble mystery—the existence of Evil in a world created and ruled by a beneficent Power. The gods have given man reason, it is said; but man abuses the gift to evil ends. "This is the fault", you say, "of men, not of the gods. As though the physician should complain of the virulence of the disease, or the pilot of the fury of the tempest! Though these are but mortal men, even in them it would seem ridiculous. Who would have asked your help, we should answer, if these difficulties had not arisen? May we not argue still more strongly in the case of the gods? The fault, you say, lies in the vices of men. But you should have given men such a rational faculty as would exclude the possibility of such crimes". He sees, as David did, "the ungodly in prosperity". The laws of Heaven are mocked, crimes are committed, and "the thunders of Olympian Jove are silent". He quotes, as it would always be easy to quote, examples of this from all history: the most telling and original, perhaps, is the retort of Diagoras, who was called the Atheist, when they showed him in the temple at Samothrace the votive tablets (as they may be seen in some foreign churches now) offered by those shipwrecked seamen who had been saved from drowning. "Lo, thou that deniest a Providence, behold here how many have been saved by prayer to the gods! " "Yea", was his reply; "but where are those commemorated who were drowned? "

The Dialogue ends with no resolution of the difficulties, and no conclusion as to the points in question. Cicero, who is the narrator of the imaginary conference, gives it as his opinion that the arguments of the Stoic seemed to him to have "the greater probability". It was the great tenet of the school which he most affected, that probability was the nearest approach that man could make to speculative truth. "We are not among those", he says, "to whom there seems to be no such thing as truth; but we say that all truths have some falsehoods attached to them which have so strong a resemblance to truth, that in such cases there is no certain note of distinction which can determine our judgment and assent. The consequence of which is that there are many things probable; and although they are not subjects of actual perception to our senses, yet they have so grand and glorious an aspect that a wise man governs his life thereby". [1] It remained for one of our ablest and most philosophical Christian writers to prove that in such matters probability was practically equivalent to demonstration. [2] Cicero's own form of scepticism in religious matters is perhaps very nearly expressed in the striking anecdote which he puts, in this dialogue, into the mouth of the Epicurean.

[Footnote 1: De Nat. Deor. i. 5.]

[Footnote 2: "To us, probability is the very guide of life". —Introd. to Butler's Analogy.]

"If you ask me what the Deity is, or what his nature and attributes are, I should follow the example of Simonides, who, when the tyrant Hiero proposed to him the same question, asked a day to consider of it. When the king, on the next day, required from him the answer, Simonides requested two days more; and when he went on continually asking double the time, instead of giving any answer, Hiero in amazement demanded of him the reason. 'Because', replied he, 'the longer I meditate on the question, the more obscure does it appear'". [1]

[Footnote 1: De Nat. Deor. i. 22.]

The position of Cicero as a statesman, and also as a member of the College of Augurs, no doubt checked any strong expression of opinion on his part as to the forms of popular worship and many particulars of popular belief. In the treatise which he intended as in some sort a sequel to this Dialogue on the 'Nature of the Gods'—that upon 'Divination'—he states the arguments for and against the national belief in omens, auguries, dreams, and such intimations of the Divine will. [1] He puts the defence of the system in the mouth of his brother Quintus, and takes himself the destructive side of the argument: but whether this was meant to give his own real views on the subject, we cannot be so certain. The course of argument employed on both sides would rather lead to the conclusion that the writer's opinion was very much that which Johnson delivered as to the reality of ghosts—"All argument is against it, but all belief is for it".

[Footnote 1: There is a third treatise, 'De Fato', apparently a continuation of the series, of which only a portion has reached us. It is a discussion of the difficult questions of Fate and Free-will.]

With regard to the great questions of the soul's immortality, and a state of future rewards and punishments, it would be quite possible to gather from Cicero's writings passages expressive of entirely contradictory views. The bent of his mind, as has been sufficiently shown, was towards doubt, and still more towards discussion; and possibly his opinions were not so entirely in a state of flux as the remains of his writings seem to show. In a future state of some kind he must certainly have believed—that is, with such belief as he would have considered the subject-matter to admit of—as a strong probability. In a speculative fragment which has come down to us, known as 'Scipio's Dream', we seem to have the creed of the man rather than the speculations of the philosopher. Scipio Africanus the elder appears in a dream to the younger who bore his name (his grandson by adoption). He shows him a vision of heaven; bids him listen to the music of the spheres, which, as they move in their order, "by a modulation of high and low sounds", give forth that harmony which men have in some poor sort reduced to notation. He bids him look down upon the earth, contracted to a mere speck in the distance, and draws a lesson of the poverty of all mere earthly fame and glory. "For all those who have preserved, or aided, or benefited their country, there is a fixed and definite place in heaven, where they shall be happy in the enjoyment of everlasting life". But "the souls of those who have given themselves up to the pleasures of sense, and made themselves, as it were, the servants of these, —who at the bidding of the lusts which wait upon pleasure have violated the laws of gods and men, —they, when they escape from the body, flit still around the earth, and never attain to these abodes but after many ages of wandering". We may gather that his creed admitted a Valhalla for the hero and the patriot, and a long process of expiation for the wicked.

There is a curious passage preserved by St. Augustin from that one of Cicero's works which he most admired—the lost treatise on 'Glory'—which seems to show that so far from being a materialist, he held the body to be a sort of purgatory for the soul.

"The mistakes and the sufferings of human life make me think sometimes that those ancient seers, or Interpreters of the secrets of heaven and the counsels of the Divine mind, had some glimpse of the truth, when they said that men are born in order to suffer the penalty for some sins committed in a former life; and that the idea is true which we find in Aristotle, that we are suffering some such punishment as theirs of old, who fell into the hands of those Etruscan bandits, and were put to death with a studied cruelty; their living bodies being tied to dead bodies, face to face, in closest possible conjunction: that so our souls are coupled to our bodies, united like the living with the dead".

But whatever might have been the theological side, if one may so express it, of Cicero's religion, the moral aphorisms which meet us here and there in his works have often in them a teaching which comes near the tone of Christian ethics. The words of Petrarch are hardly too strong—"You would fancy sometimes it was not a Pagan philosopher but a Christian apostle who was speaking". [1] These are but a few out of many which might be quoted: "Strive ever for the truth, and so reckon as that not thou art mortal, but only this thy body, for thou art not that which this outward form of thine shows forth, but each man's mind, that is the real man—not the shape which can be traced with the finger". [2] "Yea, rather, they live who have escaped from the bonds of their flesh as from a prison-house". "Follow after justice and duty; such a life is the path to heaven, and into yon assembly of those who have once lived, and now, released from the body, dwell in that place". Where, in any other heathen writer, shall we find such noble words as those which close the apostrophe in the Tusculans? —"One single day well spent, and in accordance with thy precepts, were better to be chosen than an immortality of sin! "[3] He is addressing himself, it is true, to Philosophy; but his Philosophy is here little less than the Wisdom of Scripture: and the spiritual aspiration is the same—only uttered under greater difficulties—as that of the Psalmist when he exclaims, "One day in thy courts is better than a thousand! " We may or may not adopt Erasmus's view of his inspiration—or rather, inspiration is a word which has more than one definition, and this would depend upon which definition we take; but we may well sympathise with the old scholar when he says—"I feel a better man for reading Cicero".

[Footnote 1: "Interdum non Paganum philosophum, sed apostolum loqui putes".]

[Footnote 2: 'The Dream of Scipio'.]

[Footnote 3: Tusc., v. 2.]

END OF CICERO

CPSIA information can be obtained at www.ICGtesting.com
Printed in the USA
LVOW060246140512

281575LV00006B/120/A